STOP
MAKING EXCUSES AND
START
LIVING WITH ENERGY

STOP
MAKING EXCUSES AND
START
LIVING WITH ENERGY

ALYSSA ABBEY

With illustrations by
Terry Christien Cartoonology,
www.cartoonology.com

CAPSTONE
be inspired!
™

Other Wiley Editorial Offices

John Wiley & Sons Inc., 111 River Street, Hoboken, NJ 07030, USA
Jossey-Bass, 989 Market Street, San Francisco, CA 94103-1741, USA
Wiley-VCH Verlag GmbH, Boschstr. 12, D-69469 Weinheim, Germany
John Wiley & Sons Australia Ltd, 42 McDougall Street, Milton, Queensland 4064, Australia
John Wiley & Sons (Asia) Pte Ltd, 2 Clementi Loop #02-01, Jin Xing Distripark, Singapore 129809
John Wiley & Sons Canada Ltd, 22 Worcester Road, Etobicoke, Ontario, Canada M9W 1L1

Wiley also publishes its books in a variety of electronic formats. Some content that appears in print may not be available in electronic books.

A catalogue record for this book is available from the British Library and the Library of Congress.

Library of Congress Cataloging-in-Publication Data

Abbey, Alyssa, 1965–
    Stop making excuses and start living with energy / by Alyssa Abbey.
       p.   cm.
    Includes index.
    ISBN 978-1-906465-01-8 (pbk.)
1. Excuses – Psychological aspects.   2. Self-help techniques.   3. Success – Psychological aspects.   I. Title.
    BF637.E95A23   2008
    646.7 – dc22

                                                                    2008007183

Page design by Cylinder

ISBN 13: 978-1-90646-501-8

Typeset by SNP Best-set Typesetter Ltd., Hong Kong
Printed and bound in by TJ International, Padstow, Cornwall

Substantial discounts on bulk quantities of Capstone Books are available to corporations, professional associations and other organizations. For details telephone John Wiley & Sons on (+44) 1243 770441, fax (+44) 1243 770571 or email corporatedevelopment@wiley.co.uk

Table of Contents

Acknowledgements

This book is dedicated to my loving, kind, generous, funny husband Jonathan who has encouraged and supported me in every possible way. He gives me a dose of my own medicine whenever I need it. Thank you my darling J.

And a big thank you to all of my children, especially Bryony who was chief tea maker when I needed a break myself.

I also want to thank Emma, my sterling editor, who saw the potential for this book, and her incredibly efficient assistant, Jenny for all her efforts beyond the call of duty.

Finally, thanks to Steve, my dear friend and mentor, who encouraged me not only to write this book, but to fulfil my potential in every way. He truly is a wise man who speaks the truth.

Introduction

I f you're *really* ready to bust those excuses out of your life and reclaim full-on energy, then fasten your seatbelt and get ready for a challenging ride.

We've all made excuses – that's human. And I don't want to condemn people for that. Far from it. My aim in this book is to enable you to be honest enough with yourself to get on the vitality path you want for your life, and to stay there.

I'll give you the information you need to make creative choices for your new habits. Based on 18 years' experience in energy management, I'll tell you the relevant stuff about exercise, nutrition, sleep, relaxation, relationships, positive thinking, purpose and values – all those things that relate to your energy levels – without a load of irrelevant theory, jargon or psychobabble. I know you're a busy person, so this book is succinct and to the point.

Most books on health and vitality assume that once you have a piece of information about how to improve wellbeing, you'll act on it. But we know that's not the reality. Knowing what we 'should' do does not necessarily lead to permanent, or even temporary good habits.

The shift from 'I should' . . . to 'I do' is a process, a journey. Each chapter of this book is another step in that journey, but that doesn't mean you have to work through it from start to finish. You can just do the chapters that seem relevant if it works for you.

This book is really a workbook full of questions *you* must engage in to create your own life of vitality and energy. If there's no engagement, there's no commitment. If there's no commitment, you'll just go back to all those tired excuses.

If you're prepared to make the commitment, then you can have fantastic levels of energy virtually every day of your life.

Ready?

PART I

Living with energy

" *The first principle of success is desire —
knowing what you want. Desire is the
planting of your seed.* **"**

ROBERT COLLIER (1885–1950), AUTHOR OF BESTSELLING
THE SECRET OF THE AGES

" *All the things I really like to do are
either illegal, immoral, or fattening.* **"**

ALEXANDER WOOLLCOTT (1887–1943), AUTHOR, CRITIC AND
COMMENTATOR FOR THE *NEW YORKER* MAGAZINE

CHAPTER 1

What do you really want?

You probably bought this book because you recognised from the title that you're someone who has a catalogue of what seem to be watertight excuses about why you fail to take care of yourself properly. Let's face it, we tend to be overcommitted to work (inside or outside the home), and under-committed to our own health, our families and friends, and the pursuit of happiness. It's easy to lose sight of what we really want out of life because there are **so** many demands on our time, we rarely pause to think about it. We get up each day, jump onto the treadmill we call life (currently cruising at about 90 miles per hour), and just try to hang on all day without flying off the back. We forget that there are only 24 hours in each day, and we *cannot do it all*! We have to make choices about how to spend our precious time and energy. Reading this, you might protest that you don't *really* have a choice about how you spend your time (children or relatives to care for, mortgage to be paid, deadlines at work, laundry piling up, weeds growing), but you *are* making these choices every day of your life, whether you like it or not.

The proactive life

There is a world of difference between living life in a way that you consciously choose, and simply reacting to the tasks, chores and events that come your way. That's why this first chapter is entitled: 'What do you want?' Because unless you know what you really want out of life, you won't be able to live with maximum energy. And you might spend the rest of your days with the mantra 'There's never enough time!', feeling like a Cinderella, never able to finish all those chores before you get to the fun stuff.

> **❝** *It is remarkable how many smart, highly motivated, and apparently responsible people rarely pause to contemplate their own behavior.* **❞**
> STRATFORD SHERMAN AND ALYSSA FREAS, FROM THE WILD WEST OF EXECUTIVE COACHING, *HARVARD BUSINESS REVIEW*

Let me clarify that when I talk about living the life you really want, I *do* mean taking the consequences into account. So before you point out that if you were doing what you really wanted, you'd be in the Caribbean drinking tequila and sunning yourself, let me share a story with you.

For years, my father-in-law from my first marriage made fun of my running and healthy eating. He himself had high blood pressure, a high cholesterol level and did not exercise regularly. He liked a high-fat diet, and socialising in restaurants and pubs was an important part of his life. That's what he *wanted to do*. Then he had a series of strokes and sadly ended his days aged 79 in a nursing home. Just a few months before he died, he took my hand, looked at me very intently, and though he could barely speak, said 'keep running'. I understood completely what he was saying. I felt for him so totally in that moment, and I wonder if he wished he'd lived his life differently – proactively pursuing better health.

Now, how you live your life is a personal choice, and many people insist that they would rather burn out and die young than live a 'boring' healthy longer life. That's fine, of course, if you drop dead of a heart attack and go quickly. But my father-in-law is a typical case of someone who had to spend the last five years of his life in nursing homes, unable to walk, and eventually, to speak, feed or dress himself. He died very young in my view, leaving a beautiful widow who missed him terribly.

This may seem a bit of a heavy story for an opening chapter, but my aim in this book is to help you shift your mindset about how you create energy and vitality – permanently. That won't happen by glossing over reality. Throughout the book I will provoke and challenge you constantly to examine your life, your habits and the stories you tell that limit your potential.

> *"Most people are so busy knocking themselves out trying to do everything they think they should do, they never get around to what they want to do."*
> ANONYNOMOUS

Create it!

I'm urging you now to think deeply about, articulate and visualise what you want out of life, because that is the first critical step toward getting rid of your excuses and enjoying more energy. You don't have to have perfect answers right now, just open your mind and answer the questions below, or download a clean copy from **www.stop-making-excuses.com**. I promise you it's worth the effort to create some strong images that will create a 'pull' toward the choices that will energise you and make you happy.

Why did you buy this book?

✍ ....

....

....

What would you like to have the energy for that you currently don't?

Examples: to run for a bus with ease, do some evening reading without falling asleep after the first page, take up an instrument, learn another language, play more games with your family, think creatively, or have more patience.

✍ ....

....

....

List three things currently in your life that bring you sustained happiness:

If you don't think you have three, don't worry. You will by the end of this book!

✍ ....

....

....

What other things would you like to have in your life that will make you happy?

Go on, be daring!

✍ ....

....

....

What sorts of feelings would you like to experience on a regular basis?

Examples: family love, romantic love, being respected, career fulfilment, sense of achievement, excited anticipation, contentment.

✎ ....

....

....

How fit and healthy would you like to be when you're 70? What will you look like? What activities will you do?

If you're already over 70, how about when you're 90?

✎ ....

....

....

That's it! You've just started creating your new energised life. This book will enable you to make everything you've written a reality – but **you** have to do it, because no one else will do it for you. Read on for the tools and knowledge you need . . . starting with the next fundamental question in **Chapter 2: What do you value?**

" Whatever you want to do, do it now. There are only so many tomorrows. "
UNKNOWN

" *If you don't have solid beliefs, you cannot build a stable life. Beliefs are like the foundation of a building, and they are the foundation to build your life upon.* "

ALFRED A. MONTAPERT, AUTHOR OF *SUPREME PHILOSOPHY OF LIFE: THE LAWS OF MAN*

" *Those are my principles. If you don't like them I have others.* "

GROUCHO MARX

CHAPTER 2

Connecting to what you value

One of the things that typically happens when the pressure is on, is that life becomes a treadmill that never stops. We get so busy and wrapped up in a 'to-do' list that we rarely take the time to step back and think about what is important, and *why* we're doing all this.

That's why this chapter is an exploration of what you value in life. This may seem a little odd as a way to get you to lace up your running shoes, but I believe it is vitally important that you understand what drives you, and open your eyes to the ways in which you might be living out of line with what you truly value. Along with Chapter 1, this chapter will act as a foundation for building your vitality and energy.

A basic principle of human psychology is that we go toward what we focus on – so it follows that if you want something, you must focus on it. My experience has shown that when people focus on what they *value*, and align their lives with those values, they feel happier, calmer and more fulfilled. Ultimately, they are more energised because they are not wasting so much energy on stuff which is unimportant to them.

A tremendous source of stress is living out of line with your values. It feels uncomfortable, and the niggling discomfort grows over time until you are completely out of balance and ill (in body, mind or spirit). This is because the things we value are always floating in our subconscious mind and influencing us whether we acknowledge them or not. When we do pay attention to what they are, we can shape them and live by them.

So what are values exactly?

Values are the things we would not want to live without – the things we hold dear. They can be virtues such as honesty and integrity, generosity or courage. They can be aspects of personality like a sense of humour or enthusiasm. Or they can be irreplaceable things like family, friends, health or inner peace.

On the following pages is a worksheet that will help you to examine and articulate your values, as well as a list of commonly held values. This list is not intended to be prescriptive, but purely to help your thinking about what is really important to you. If you do no other exercise in this book, I would suggest you do this one. Many of my clients have told me that this was the best thing they ever did for self-understanding. Others have come back to me to say that it was an incredibly useful source of guidance when faced with difficult decisions or challenging times.

I suggest that you take at least 30 minutes to sit quietly alone, in a comfortable, peaceful place, in order to think through these questions. There are no easy answers, no right answers. This is about you and what is really important in your (one and only) life. When you complete them, you might wish to copy your list of values into your diary, filofax, palm pilot or blackberry, and make a point of referring to them once a month or even every week! When you do, ask yourself, 'Am I living my values?' If you live what you value, you will be living with energy!

SHAPING YOUR VALUES

Virtues – Personality traits – Loved ones – Irreplaceable things

To formulate ideas about what your values are, work through the following questions, and then list your top 5–10 values. Answer here or download a clean copy from **www.stop-making-excuses.com**.

What qualities do you exhibit when you are at your best?

Examples: caring, vivacious, energetic, enthusiastic, relaxed, patient, loving, entertaining, giving, fun, professional, efficient, empathic, intelligent, creative.

✎...

....

....

What special gifts do you bring to the world?

✎...

....

....

What is your definition of success?

✎...

....

....

When you come to the end of your life, what will be the three most important lessons you learned?

1. ....

....

....

2. ....

....

....

3. ....

....

....

What do you value most in life? List your values, and then at least two ways that you will live those values.

For example, if you list Love as a value, how will you express it? Perhaps by making sure you tell your partner or child every day how much you love them, or by setting aside one evening per week to do something special with them.

1 ....

....

....

2 ....

....

....

3 ....

....

....

4 ....

....

....

5 ....

....

....

6 ....

....

....

7 ....

....

....

8 ....

....

....

9 ....

....

....

10 ....

....

....

Commonly held values

Achievement	Fast-paced work
Advancement and promotion	Financial gain
Adventure	Forgiveness
Affection	Freedom
Arts	Friendships
Challenging problems	Fun
Change and variety	Growth
Close relationships	Health
Community	Helping other people
Competence	Helping society
Competition	Honesty
Contribution	Independence
Cooperation	Influencing others
Country	Inner peace
Creativity	Integrity
Decisiveness	Intellectual status
Democracy	Involvement
Ecological awareness	Job satisfaction
Economic security	Job security
Effectiveness	Knowledge
Efficiency	Leadership
Ethical practice	Location
Excellence	Love
Excitement	Loyalty
Expertise	Market position
Fairness	Meaningful work
Fame	Merit
Family	Money
Fast living	Nature

Order (stability, conformity)	Responsibility and accountability
Openness	Security
Personal development (living up	Self-respect
to one's fullest potential)	Serenity
Physical challenge	Stability
Pleasure	Status
Power and authority	Supervising others
Privacy	Tranquillity
Public service	Truth
Purity	Variety
Quality of what I take part in	Vitality
Quality relationships	Wealth
Recognition	Wisdom
Religion	Working under pressure
Reputation	Working with others
Respect	Working alone

It's not what you say, it's what you do

Mike came to me for coaching explaining that he felt stressed, exhausted and unable to work to his full potential. To the outside world, he still looked fine. He was good-looking, reasonably fit, and had the clothes, house and car that matched his six-figure salary. But during the previous six months he had begun to develop stomach trouble, chronic fatigue and occasional tingling in his fingers and toes. Both a neurologist and a gastroenterologist could find nothing wrong with him. He had taken three weeks off work to try to recover some energy, but as soon as he was back at work, the symptoms returned.

As we talked, the deep unhappiness began to show on his face. He revealed that he hated his job and the people he worked with, and that he had been homesick ever since moving abroad to take this position that was only meant to be for a year.

'How long have you been working here?' I asked.

'For ten years', was his reply.

'Ten years? And what sort of hours do you work?'

He said it varied between 55 and 70 per week.

'How much longer are you going to spend here in this country, in this job?'

He replied that he didn't really have any exit plans from either. His reasons? Well, he earned a considerable salary, and there were great educational opportunities for his daughter. He maintained that the most important thing in the world to him was his family's happiness. I asked him how long he thought his family could remain happy with the situation as it was. That was when he began to realise that there was a vast gap between what he truly valued: the love of his wife and child, fitness and health, travel and adventure, making a contribution to society – and the reality of his life. He slowly came to understand that only by living his values could he create a foundation for his health to stand on.

It was a big step, but he made the decision to reduce his hours (and his income) in order to spend more time with his family, travel more and have more fun. He has made a whole range of changes to his diet and fitness habits, and is dedicating ten minutes a day to total relaxation. This was particularly important for his recovery because he used to spend just about every waking minute in 'go' mode. Because he had become so exhausted, regaining his full energy levels took nearly a year. He no longer has any debilitating symptoms, and he feels a sense of vitality that had been absent for too long.

Mike's story shows how easy it is to lose touch with your values, and to become 'acclimatised' to a life that is slowly making you ill and unhappy. It can happen so gradually you don't notice the loss of vitality and sense of purpose. Mike had to go back to absolute basics to move forward on a new path that is both sustainable and enjoyable.

*" Life begets life. Energy creates energy.
It is by spending oneself that one
becomes rich. "*

SARAH BERNHARDT (1844–1923), FRENCH STAGE ACTRESS,
MEMBER OF THE LEGION OF HONOUR

*" People often say that motivation doesn't
last. Well, neither does bathing – that's
why we recommend it daily. "*

ZIG ZIGLAR, AUTHOR, TOP SALESMAN AND
MOTIVATIONAL SPEAKER

CHAPTER 3

The four energies

I suspect that when you examined your values in the last chapter, you discovered that they are about much more than a moral compass or a set of behavioural traits. They probably encompass health, relationships, career, mental development and charitable pursuits too.

It is also true of energy levels that it's not just about one thing. People usually associate energy with physical endurance but energy flows in more than one currency. In fact, there are four distinct types I want to explain to you. Now that you've thought about what your values are, it's time to understand something about the energy you need to *live* those values.

Understanding the four energies

Imagine you've had a tough day at work with a long meeting where colleagues didn't agree with your ideas. You've had to defend your stance, and there were no allies to help. You get home drained and tired – but is this physical fatigue? Not really. You sat on your backside most of the day. Could it be that you're just mentally and emotionally drained?

Now imagine a second scenario: You're physically in great shape, and all the relationships in your life are positive. But, you're bored at work, you have virtually no career or personal goals and no guiding vision for your life. Is it possible you'd feel lethargic and somewhat depressed? The reason: a lack of mental and spirit energy.

The four types of energy are: **_Physical, Mental, Emotional and Spirit_**. If you develop an awareness of which of these four energy currencies you might be lacking, you'll be able to do the most effective thing to top up . . . rather than lumping them all together as just 'energy' and having a single strategy for energy renewal – such as vegging out in front of the TV!

The four energies

Below is a clear and succinct definition of each of the four energies – enough for you to fully understand without becoming theory-heavy! Along with that I've given just an overview of the sorts of strategies that build these energies. **Part III – Vitality Now!**, has lots more on how to maximise them.

Mental Energy

Mental energy has to do with alertness and concentration, learning, analysis, logical process, creativity and intuition. We feel it as mental sharpness, creative 'flow', challenge, certainty, and even 'eureka!' With high levels of mental energy you can easily move between the detail of a project and a wider perspective, and between external and internal focus. The four most important things you can do to maintain mental energy are:

1. Set clear goals and objectives
2. Be disciplined over where your time is spent

3. Train your brain like an athlete trains muscles: challenge it consistently, but schedule regular downtime to rest it and regain power for the next mental bout

4. Regularly engage in activities that stimulate your creativity.

Emotional Energy

Do you know someone who lights up the room when they walk in? I hope so. Now, do you know someone who lights up the room when they walk out? If you can 'get' this, you can begin to understand what emotional energy feels like. It can be hard to put your finger on, but you know when someone makes you feel good, and when they don't.

Emotional energy comes from relationships that give you positive feelings, connection, teamwork and collaboration. It feels like fulfilment, satisfaction, warmth, happiness, and being valued, liked and loved. You can create more emotional energy by:

1. Building self-awareness, self-confidence and self-control
2. Feeling empathy and seeking to understand others
3. Ensuring others feel valued and developed
4. Motivating and influencing others
5. Giving your love and energy freely.

Spirit Energy

Spirit energy is about inspiration, aspiration, enthusiasm, future vision and possibility, optimism, hope, joy and meaning to life. It is experienced in many different ways for different people: as a god or a higher being in the universe, a higher purpose of life, or as unswerving principles, truths or values about how to live your life. As with emotional energy, it is associated with peace and love. Capturing spirit energy is also highly individual, but some conduits may be:

1. Developing perspective on life and what gives happiness
2. Understanding today in the context of a wider life and time-line

3. Living your values
4. Personal development, growth and learning
5. Relaxation, meditation, prayer and time out in nature
6. Seeking to understand the meaning of life
7. Seeking a higher meaning for *your* life
8. The ability to be playful and laugh.

Physical Energy

Physical energy is represented by the Four 'S's:

Stamina
Strength
Suppleness
Speed

It's a relaxed bodily readiness, quickness, lightness, feelings of physical confidence and wellness. Physical energy is the one we tend to understand the best, but fail to do the things we know would increase it. It is best maintained by uncompromised rituals (there's no getting around this) that enable:

1. Good quality sleep
2. Regular relaxation
3. Good nutrition (including limited caffeine and alcohol – and zero nicotine)
4. Physical exercise that enhances cardiovascular endurance, strength, flexibility and speed.

Some people see these things as a tortuous life sentence of being a 'health freak' and having no fun. It really depends on your perspective. You could view these habits as difficult, painful or boring, or you could view them as your way of getting a vital energy source that will enable you to achieve what you want in life – whether that is winning a tennis match or getting a promotion.

Physical energy is also about what we experience through our senses – the sights, smells, sounds, tastes and touch we encounter each day. That's why your environment has such a profound impact on your energy levels.

Sustaining the four energies

There is no one formula for building and sustaining these four energy currencies. Each of us must find workable *and enjoyable* ways of maintaining energy and vitality. Yours will be as individual as you are, and remember that you are allowed to have fun!

Sometimes we just need a quick energy fix, and there are lots of ideas for **'Instant Revitalisation'** at the end of this chapter. This 'pin-up' can also be printed from the website **www.stop-making-excuses.com**. Underpinning these quick fixes, we need to cultivate a range of habits that will keep energy high week after week, and give us the long-term health that we would probably like to enjoy! Again, **Part III – Vitality Now!** is devoted to energy strategies, with heaps of practical ways to develop and maintain *all four energies.*

The currencies are connected

Ever notice how, when you exercise, you not only feel physically better, but emotionally higher and mentally sharper? That's because the four energies are connected. When you work on one, you get more of the others, too. Other examples you might have noticed are: feeling proud improves your posture, a burning desire enhances creativity, working creatively can increase patience, finishing a mental task brings feelings of satisfaction or fulfilment.

You can download a colourful copy of the following Live with Energy pin-up from **www.stop-making-excuses.com**.

> *Energy and persistence alter all things.*
> BENJAMIN FRANKLIN

LIVE WITH ENERGY PIN-UP

Instant revitalisation

Quick ways to get energy when you're flagging

Take a moment to assess what you most need right now. Are you lacking physical, mental, emotional or spirit energy?

Physical energy

- Have a break! Get away from your work
- Straighten your back, lift your breastbone, drop your shoulders
- Have a drink of water or refreshing herbal tea. Try lemon/orange/ginger/ginseng/cinnamon/liquorice
- Top up your fuel level – with something sustaining
- Have an aromatherapy break. Put 5–8 drops of your chosen essential oil in a container of hot water, and soak in the scent.

60-second relaxation

- Sit comfortably with good posture
- Close your eyes/Breathe calmly from your belly
- Mentally check for areas of muscular tension
- Imagine letting go of that tension
- Visualise a relaxing scene
- Say a word to yourself on each exhalation that expresses your peaceful feeling ('calm', 'peace', 'relax').

60-second supercharge

Prepare as in 60-second relaxation, then recall a scene in which you were feeling energised and exhilarated. Visualise the scene, and re-run the feelings associated with it. Say a word to yourself on each exhalation that sums up the feelings ('wow', 'energy', 'electric', 'supercharged'). This will create a powerful association that you can use by simply saying the word to yourself anytime for a quick energy recharge.

Mental energy

- Reconsider what you are presently doing. Is it the best use of your time?
- Enjoy 5 minutes of pleasure reading
- Right now, do you have more optimistic or more pessimistic thoughts in your head? Do you need to change the balance?
- Is the pressure you feel external or internal? Assess your expectations of yourself and ask if you are expecting something superhuman or unachievable
- Are you distracted by something? Either deal with it right now to get it out of your head, or write it on a list somewhere and mentally *put it aside*
- Set a time limit on the task you are working on if it is an unpleasant one. Promise yourself to work on it for x number of minutes, with a reward at the end.

Emotional energy

- Phone a friend. Just a 2-minute call to get some energy, and to give them a positive message, too
- Send a loving text to your partner, child or friend
- Ask for help. Brainstorm who could help you, and phone them right now
- Have a laugh. Try: www.laughlab.co.uk or www.comedy-zone.net
- Consider what your feelings are right at this moment. Are you sad, angry, resentful, afraid, stressed? If it is a negative emotion, consider letting go of it, and replacing it with a positive one. Could you be forgiving, grateful, peaceful, sympathetic, brave, passionate, committed?
- Think about your impact on others right now. How would you like to be impacting on them?

Spirit energy

- Reconnect to your overall purpose. Is what you are doing now getting you there in some way?
- Slip on some headphones and listen to 5 minutes of uplifting music
- Read your affirmations. If you don't have any, write one! See **Chapter 13 – Affirmations and celebrations**

" If people around you aren't going anywhere, if their dreams are no bigger than hanging out on the corner, or if they're dragging you down, get rid of them. Negative people can sap your energy so fast, and they can take your dreams from you, too. "

EARVIN "MAGIC" JOHNSON

" Hard work never killed anybody, but I figure why take the chance? "

EDGAR BERGEN (1903–1978),
AMERICAN ACTOR AND VENTRILOQUIST

CHAPTER 4

Energy sources and sappers

In order for you to get and sustain the energy you want, you've got to be aware of the things that are currently draining you of valuable energy. You might say you're already well aware of those, but you can learn a lot by scrutinising them. It helps you get to a place where you're ready to do something about them.

You, the vitality vessel

To be more aware of your own energy levels, you can think of yourself as a vitality vessel, or a big bucket of energy. Every day you need to dip into the bucket to do the things you want to do, and every day you do things to replenish the energy, like sleep and eat. If you look at the diagram, you'll see that there are lots of ideas on the left hand side about how to top up your vitality, and you could probably add some of your own. On the right hand side, you'll see a list of typical things we do

Vitality Vessel

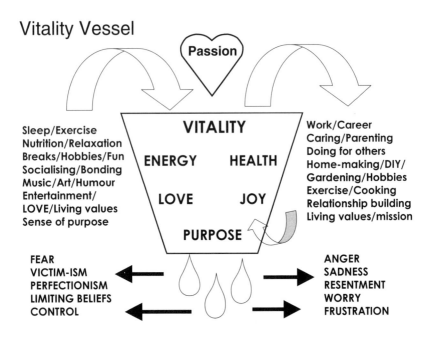

that require energy – though some of them also have a positive feedback of actually bringing in more energy in the long run, like exercise or charitable work.

Also look at the drips coming from the bottom of the bucket, and think about which ones apply to you. We all have some energy leakage, and although it's all part of being human, we can work toward minimising it.

Notice that the magic ingredient that goes into the mix is **passion**, because unless you're getting fired up by what's going on in your life, no amount of ticking the right wellbeing boxes is going to make you feel energised.

At the end of **Part III – Vitality Now!** you'll be creating your own individual energy vessel with your formula for keeping it filled to the brim. For now, I want you to complete the following Vitality questionnaire that will help you diagnose where you're staying topped up, and where you're not.

Your Vitality

For each question, circle the percentage that best describes your energy level out of 100% for that particular area of your life, or most closely describes your habits in that area. You can fill in the questionnaire here, or download a clean copy from **www.stop-making-excuses.com**.

1. Overall, how are your energy levels today?

I'm running on empty				I'm ready for anything
20% 40%	60%		80%	100%

2. Physically, how do you feel?

Shattered				Fighting fit
20% 40%	60%		80%	100%

3. What about emotionally?

I need chocolate/ a hug/to scream				I'm on top of the world!
20% 40%	60%		80%	100%

4. What's your concentration like?

Can't focus on anything				Razor-sharp
20% 40%	60%		80%	100%

5. How motivated do you feel?

Who cares?				Fired up
20%	40%	60%	80%	100%

6. When you wake up in the morning, how do you feel most frequently?

Like pulling the covers back over my head				Rested and refreshed
20%	40%	60%	80%	100%

7. Do you follow a healthy diet each day?

I'm on first name terms with the local takeaway				It's a way of life
20%	40%	60%	80%	100%

8. Do you resort to junk food (crisps, chocolate etc.) to keep your energy levels up?

All the time				Never
20%	40%	60%	80%	100%

9. Do you use caffeine to keep your energy levels up?

Addict				Never touch it
20%	40%	60%	80%	100%

10. Do you drink 2L of water each day?

If I'm honest? Never				Habitually
20%	40%	60%	80%	100%

11. Which best describes your alcohol consumption?

More than recommended every day	More than recommended 3 times per week or a weekly binge	More than recommended once a week or occasional binge	I stick to recom- mended levels	Teetotal
20%	40%	60%	80%	100%

* 1 unit of alcohol = ½ pint of beer, 25 ml of spirit or a 175 ml glass of wine

** Recommended daily consumption not to exceed for Men = 3 units and for Women = 2 units

12. Do you use a relaxation technique such as meditation or breathing exercises?

Never	Monthly or in a crisis	Fortnightly	Weekly	Daily
20%	40%	60%	80%	100%

13. Do you exercise?

Never knowingly	Very occasionally	I do, but it's sporadic	1–2 times a week religiously	3+ times a week it's a way of life
20%	40%	60%	80%	100%

14. Do you laugh often?

Less than once a day				More than 6 × a day
20%	40%	60%	80%	100%

15. Are you happy?

I'm on a pretty low ebb				I choose to be happy every day
20%	40%	60%	80%	100%

16. Do you have peace of mind?

Not really				Completely
20%	40%	60%	80%	100%

17. Do you know – really know – what your values are?

Never thought about it				Absolutely
20%	40%	60%	80%	100%

18. Do you live those values?

I don't have time				Yes, I use them to guide my decisions
20%	40%	60%	80%	100%

19. How well do you maintain concentration during the day?

Sorry, what?				Very well
20%	40%	60%	80%	100%

20. Do you take regular breaks?

Ha! Ha! Don't have time				Like clockwork
20%	40%	60%	80%	100%

21. Do you have an interest outside of work that you pursue on a regular basis?

No	Monthly	Fortnightly	Weekly	Daily
20%	40%	60%	80%	100%

22. Do your relationships give you energy or drain your energy?

Majority drain energy				Majority give energy
20%	40%	60%	80%	100%

23. Do you actively develop and strengthen your relationships?

I don't have time /don't know how				I make the effort every day
20%	40%	60%	80%	100%

24. How valued do you feel by your family, friends, work team or community?

Not at all				Completely
20%	40%	60%	80%	100%

25. Do you take part in charity or community projects/events which lift your spirits?

No, never				Yes, regularly
20%	40%	60%	80%	100%

To score this questionnaire, work out your average percentage by adding all the scores together and dividing by 25.

If you scored:

70–100%

You are highly energised and focussed, and most likely you feel pretty jazzed about life! What do you need to do to keep the fire burning? If you reached this score but don't feel energised enough, it's because your expectations are higher, and that's super. Work through **Part III – Vitality Now!** for ideas about how to raise your energy through the roof.

50–69%

You have some energy, but it probably feels like an effort to get going on things, whether it's work or physical activities. If you want to feel better, you need to discover more sources of renewal, and make them happen in your life. Feel too tired to make any changes? Do something small to boost your energy enough to think about the bigger things.

Below 50%

You're in survival mode in terms of your energy, and it's probably diffi-cult to concentrate or find the oomph for new projects or anything proactive. If you feel you're hanging on for dear life, don't despair! This is not a life-sentence if you take some positive steps – small ones at first, and one thing at a time. What could you do first? Celebrate the fact that you're reading this book – it's full of ideas and motivation to get you out of the doldrums.

I hope this questionnaire raised your awareness of where you might need to focus your efforts for sustaining energy levels. You'll be developing your formula for boundless energy at the end of **Part III – Vitality Now!** But first, we're going to name and shame your excuses in **Part II – No More Excuses!**, until all you can do is fall down laughing at them.

> " *The higher your energy level, the more efficient your body. The more efficient your body, the better you feel and the more you will use your talent to produce outstanding results.* "
> ANTHONY ROBBINS

No more excuses

" *You will never find time for anything.*
If you want time you must make it."

ANONYMOUS

" *I had a secretarial job but I called in*
sick a lot. I would say I had 'female
troubles'. My boss didn't know I
meant her."

WENDY LIEBMAN, COMEDIAN

CHAPTER 5

Excuses, excuses

We all justify the way we live our lives, don't we? Not many people say things like, 'I know I should exercise, and I just make up excuses all the time as to why I don't, to make myself feel better.' Nope. Instead we excuse ourselves because of some circumstance or other. It's not difficult. Just remember that if mass murderers can justify their actions (and they generally do), then justifying skipping the gym is always going to be a piece of cake!

The top 10

In 18 years of educating, coaching and facilitating workshops on health, stress management and vitality, I have heard just about every excuse in the book about why people don't develop energy-giving habits. Below I've listed the 10 excuses I hear most often, plus a few of the more bizarre ones just to give you a few laughs. As you read, be honest with yourself about which ones you use. Hopefully, you can begin to laugh at yourself, because that's another good step toward getting past those excuses to a life of boundless energy.

1. **'I don't have time'** is the absolute number one most used excuse. If I had a penny for every time I've heard this one, I'd be a very wealthy woman. It's easy to use this as an excuse because we truly are extremely busy. We rationalise that if we have **so** much to do, we've got to take the pressure off somewhere. It's only fair that we shouldn't have to fit in all that healthy living stuff when we're trying to **make** a living, right? I had a client who was adamant that she didn't have time to eat even a banana during her working day, (interesting though, that she did have time to eat chocolate bars). She was so convinced that the reason for her poor diet was lack of time that she didn't see the irony of her own reasoning. A colleague of mine had a client who, when asked if she could practise breathing in a calmer way throughout the day to lower her stress levels, said she didn't have time to breathe like that. The real story is that you have time for everything that is truly important to you. I have never met anyone who, when absolutely determined to put a habit in place because it was vitally important to them, did not manage, somehow, to accomplish it.

2. **'I'll do it when'** is really just a variation on the 'I don't have time' theme. So many people delude themselves that when this project is finished, or when a child starts nursery – then they will have time. But funnily enough, life just never seems to slow down. The 'I'll do it when' theme is great for satisfying friends or partners who are encouraging you to do something to look after yourself. I often hear this from smokers who say they couldn't possibly quit smoking in the midst of this busy period at work – they'll quit when they take a vacation. But come the vacation, they allow themselves 'this last week of pleasure', and promise to give up when they go back to work! Health, relaxation, happiness and fun can be delayed endlessly, but the body still keeps score. You need balance and nurturing all the time, more so when life gets busy.

3. **I tried it and it didn't work.** I've heard this applied to attempts to diet, meditate, exercise, build team spirit at work – you name it. Ultimately, this is merely a way to absolve yourself of responsibility. The thought process goes something like this: 'I've tried this thing to make me feel better or healthier, and it didn't work, so I don't have to try again or do anything else – it's *not my fault.*' Literally every time I've heard this excuse, and questioned the person further, there's very little evidence he or she tried for very long. I had a client recently say she could not relax no matter what she tried. I asked her what she'd done and she proudly said she had taken a course in meditation. So the next question was, 'how long have you been practising it?' and it turned out she had only stuck at it for a week after the course. Because she found her mind drifted, she decided relaxation was impossible. When I told her that Zen masters find their minds drift too, she got a different perspective. Another funny example was a guy in a workshop who didn't want to try any of the herbal teas I had brought along. He said he 'didn't get on' with herbal teas. I asked him which ones he'd tried, and then he admitted that he had never tried *any!* His mantra that all herbal teas are horrible allowed him to feel okay about his 10 cups of coffee a day. Even though he has never even tried any, he can reassure himself that it's not his fault he drinks so much coffee. He doesn't have a choice, does he?

4. **'I can't change'** in its many forms is hugely popular as an excuse. I hear things like 'I've never been much of an athlete', 'I've always had a sweet tooth', 'I'm not creative', 'My brain goes 'round and 'round and I can't focus', and even 'I'm just no good at relationships'. The real story is usually that there is a fear of change because of a fear of failure or rejection. Just like excuse #3, this is another great way of relinquishing responsibility for your life and placing it at the feet of bad luck, genetics or whatever. If you 'can't change,' then again, it's not your fault. What a relief. Now you don't have

to do anything else! This excuse can also reveal a genuine belief that change is impossible, like a woman I coached recently about her incessant worrying. We discussed a number of tools for reprogramming her thinking, but ultimately she did not *believe* that any of them could work for her. Some people never learn that like Dorothy in the *Wizard of Oz*, they had the power all along to do what they wanted. It's just a case of clicking those red shoes together – and believing you can. In **Chapters 10–13** there are some tools to help shift your beliefs.

> " *Life is not holding a good hand; life is playing a poor hand well.* "
> DANISH PROVERB

5. **I'm not really that bad.** It's a denial thing. We've all been there. There will always be someone who is more overweight or less fit, a heavier drinker or smoker than you. If you use them to make yourself feel better you're deluding yourself. Don't get sucked into comparisons of yourself either to less energetic, or more energetic (fit, healthy) people. What really matters is how *you* feel, and what you know to be true when you look in the mirror.

6. **'It's too late'** is a derivative of 'I can't change', but important to mention in its own right because I have seen quite a number of clients over 50 who are convinced that any change in lifestyle or mental habits at this point will not make any difference to the

quality of their lives. We'll see in **Chapter 11 – Banish mental gremlins** that you must be very careful what you tell yourself repeatedly. If you're repeating, 'Well, I'm getting older so it's not surprising that I'm stiffer, or weaker, or slower,' that that will become your reality. And what a load of twaddle! There are enough stories out there of grannies deciding to run marathons or returning to university, to prove that the body and brain will respond at any time to the right nurturing. It's only too late when you are on your deathbed.

> " *Whatever limits us we call fate.* "
> RALPH WALDO EMERSON

7. **'It's boring! If I live in such a healthy way, I'll never have any fun.'** I always tell my clients that having fun is one of the best sources of energy there is. You just might need to adjust your beliefs about what's boring and what's fun – as well as a little look into the future to see how fun it will be to lack mobility or be in pain. You could have fun socialising without so much alcohol, couldn't you (possibly even more fun)? You can have fun doing the physical activities that you like rather than those you loathe. You can have a great time cooking fresh, healthful food. What's so fun about eating rubbish that doesn't nourish you?

8. **'Even if I live healthily, I might still die young of some disease, or get hit by a bus tomorrow'.** Yeeess. Or you could live to be 90.

9. **'I don't have the resources'**: space, money, knowledge, equipment. Once I had a funny conversation with a client about how she might get some exercise into her life, because her lack of fitness was impacting on her ability to walk up stairs or even do a day's shopping. She insisted that she was afraid to exercise outdoors so that was out of the question (bear in mind she did go out for other things). And she said that she lived in such a small house that exercising indoors was impossible – even on a mini trampoline that I suggested. And of course she couldn't afford

to join a gym (didn't I know how little accounts clerks earn?). I'm quite certain that if someone bought her a gym, she could come up with a reason why she could not use it herself. I also sometimes hear that eating healthily is too expensive. Don't even get me started on that one. Plenty of my clients have clearly never done a price comparison between seasonable vegetables, fruits, beans and rice vs ready-made meals, pizza and ice cream. You don't have to eat blueberries in January to have all the energy you want.

10. **'It hurts! Exercise just makes me tired/ill/injured.'** If exercise makes you tired it is only because you are so unfit. Anyone can see the difference in vitality and vibrancy between marathon runners and couch potatoes. The thing is, during the first four weeks of any exercise programme, the body is adapting to the new demands placed on it, and will protest. Of course you need to take it steadily and sensibly. If it hurts, ensure your technique is correct, or reduce the intensity, or find a different exercise that doesn't hurt.

Other excuses you might have tried

'There's not enough daylight.' When the days get shorter in winter I start to hear from clients that it's impossible to go out for a bike ride or even a walk. Hello! There are thousands of exercises you can do indoors. It's instinctive to conserve energy in the winter, but we've got to overcome this and do the opposite in order to keep energy levels up!

'I can't go to the gym looking like this.' And you think you're invisible when you're not at the gym?

" It is easier to offer objections than it is to get busy. "
ANONYMOUS

'I don't know how to work all that equipment at the gym.' This one is really grasping at straws.

'I absolutely can't concentrate unless I eat chocolate.' At first I thought this client was joking, but he wasn't!

'My family comes first.' If you love them, you'll keep yourself healthy.

*I think you get the message here. Now you're ready to do the questionnaire in **Chapter 6** to expose your own excuses!*

" *Most people can do extraordinary things if they have the confidence or take the risks. Yet most people don't. They sit in front of the telly and treat life as if it goes on forever.* "

PHILIP ANDREW ADAMS, AUSTRALIAN PUBLIC
COMMENTATOR AND BROADCASTER, CREATOR OF
SUCCESSFUL 'LIFE, BE IN IT' CAMPAIGN

" *— I wish I had time for a hobby.
— Norm, you've got time to make your
own coal.* "

NORM PETERSON AND CLIFF CLAVIN, '*CHEERS*'

CHAPTER 6

What's really stopping you?

Now it's time to 'name and shame' *your* excuses. Deep down, you know the reasons for not doing what's best for you in the long run. To help articulate them, fill in the following worksheet (or download a clean copy from **www.stop-making-excuses.com**), and *be honest*. If you aren't, you'll just end up back in the same negative loop – wanting to look after yourself and knowing you *should*, but not doing it because of some justification that works for you every time.

What are your worst health habits?

Examples: lack of exercise, too much chocolate, alcohol or junk food, smoking, lack of sleep.

✎ ....

....

What are the good health habits you have that you only do occasionally?

Examples: exercise, relaxation, meditation, lots of fruits & vegetables, getting enough sleep, pampering yourself. Be as specific as possible.

✎ ....

....

What are your excuses?

Review the excuses listed in Chapter 5. Write down which ones you use, even if only occasionally, *using the words you use in your head or out loud as closely as possible.* For example: Your personal variation of 'I don't have time' might be, 'I can't go to yoga tonight because I've got to do the Tesco on-line order, and if I don't get that done, we won't have any food in the house this weekend.'

✎ ....

....

Now, for your each of your *bad health habits*, write a counter-statement to the excuse you commonly use.

For example: Yoga is critically important to my fitness and wellbeing. I will put it above everything that is not just as important to my health. Or, something simple like: Quality Sleep, Fewer Wrinkles.

✎ ....

....

For each of your *good health habits you don't do often enough*, write a counter-statement to the excuse you commonly use to excuse this.

For example: My body uses the fuel I give it *every* day. I will give it wholesome food *every* day, There's all the time in the world, or Exercise is fun if I make it fun.

✎ ....

....

From these counter-statements you've just written, choose the 1 or 2 that you MOST need to hear repeatedly until they stick. Now write them in *big*, **bold** letters and stick them up on your refrigerator, by your bathroom mirror or in your car. **DO IT NOW** before you do anything else. This is critically important! If you don't take any action as a result of reading this, you'll have had a pleasant, informative read and no more.

> " *Reduce your plan to writing. The moment you complete this, you will have definitely given concrete form to the intangible desire.* "
> NAPOLEON HILL

These statements are **AFFIRMATIONS**, and you'll be writing more of them in **Chapter 13 – Affirmations and celebrations**. Keep them in place for a minimum of three weeks, and say them to yourself or out loud at least three times each day.

> " *Habits are at first cobwebs, then cables.* "
> SPANISH PROVERB

Committing to action

At the end of my workshops, I have delegates write commitment letters to themselves. I then post these letters back to the writers three months later, as a reminder or to prod them if they haven't taken any action yet. As you can imagine, people write all sorts of different things, and I've picked out a selection of actual letters to show you what people commit to as a result of spending a day thinking about their own energy management – and how they're living their lives. In **Part IV – Action Plans That You Actually Take Action On** you'll have a chance to make your commitments, but you don't have to wait. If you get inspired by these letters, write your own, and give it to a friend with instructions to give it back to you three months from now.

Dear C,

How are you? I am fine. Right! Enough chit-chat let's get down to business! There's 3 things you've got to do to improve yourself and your life. You know what they are but you need reminding!

1. Stop being so lazy – get a job/promotion
2. Do more exercise you fat git.
3. Pay more attention to the wife – less internet poker/xbox. Stop walking away from the troubles in your life.

Your pal,

C

****

Dear A,

You are capable

You are beautiful

Are you drinking more water and fewer energy drinks? You did promise, you know.

I hope you have learnt to relax and clear your mind, and realise tomorrow is another day.

Believe in yourself and you will be what you want to be. X

****

Dear M,

I hope that when you get this note that you will be happier, healthier and more at peace with yourself. You are a wonderful, brilliant person and you deserve to be happy. I'm going to have the courage to look after myself first in the next 3 months. This weekend I'm going to make a plan for myself and then follow it through!

****

Dear D,

When you get this letter you will have accepted where you are in life and become happy with what today will give you. In practical terms you will have made steps at work to enable you to become engaged in work which excites you, motivates you and fits with your values. You are truly too blessed to be stressed.

****

Dear Y,
Your objectives were:
Give up smoking on 1/11/05
Reduce your alcohol intake
Exercise: extra walking, skipping and gardening
Bedtime should be at 10!
Work: ask for what you want. Do something about your proposed role!

****

Well done you!
You have finally managed to delegate more work and trust others. Doesn't it all make sense?

****

Dear I,
I hope you are enjoying life more and stressing less about what more to achieve. Just relax and enjoy the journey through life.
Whatever comes your way is for a reason. Don't take things so seriously.
Try to meditate at least 15 mins every other day and try to do something different every week.
Ps. Don't forget your friends

Does any of this hit the mark for your life? Where do you need to be more honest with yourself about how you are caring for yourself?

" *Pay no attention to what the critics say; no statue has ever been put up for a critic.* "

JEAN SIBELIUS, CELEBRATED FINNISH COMPOSER

" *When I hear someone sigh, 'Life is hard,' I am always tempted to ask 'Compared to what?'* "

SYDNEY HARRIS, JOURNALIST

CHAPTER 7

Mind your language

If you really want to bust your tired, sad excuses for not developing more energy, you've got to start paying attention to the language you use:

* when you talk about your wellness habits
* when you describe yourself and your abilities.

So what things am I alluding to? There are a whole range of words, phrases and criticisms that bring your energy and your horizons down. They also perpetuate your excuses. If we could become more aware of how that language infiltrates our subconscious minds, we might be more careful about what we utter.

For instance, do you say (or even think) 'I *have* to go to the gym now', or 'Being on a diet is *so hard*. I can't eat anything'? How about, 'I *hate* accounting' or 'I *must* get all the work done'?

Let's start with 'I can't', which I hear a lot. 'I can't relax', 'I can't exercise', 'I can't function without caffeine', even 'I can't cope'. Most of us know that when you say I can't, it becomes a self-fulfilling prophesy, but is there an area of your life where you're still using this phrase?

Next, if you want to affect your life positively, I urge you to stop saying 'I should' or 'I'll try to' do this or that. Whenever I hear these phrases, I know the person has no real intention of taking any action whatsoever. Think of the times you've said 'I should exercise more', 'I should eat less junk food', 'I'll try to relax', 'I'll try to get out to concerts more with my friends'. When you say 'I should' or 'I'll try', your subconscious mind hears '. . . but I don't really have to, it's not imperative, I can justify not doing it.' Only when you use language such as 'I will', and simultaneously think 'this IS going to happen', can you start the ball rolling toward real, effective action.

Another thing to look out for in your conversations with yourself and others is 'I have to'. Whenever you *have* to do something, you resent it. If you *choose* it, you're happy about it. It's a hundred times more energising when you choose. I recently witnessed a good example of the difference between these attitudes in my yoga class. On the first class after the summer break, there were a noticeable number of people who were moaning about getting back to doing back bends, abdominal work, literally everything we were practising. Without actually saying the words, these people were asking 'Do we have to?' I noticed that the moaners were the people who really hadn't made much progress in their yoga in the last year, and I almost wanted to ask them, 'Well, why are you here?' If it's to increase flexibility or strength, or to relax, then why wouldn't you embrace the postures our wonderful teacher is giving us? Others in the class who enjoy the challenge and expect to do some work to get results are the ones who have moved forward considerably. So, if you're saying 'I have to' often, you might be hindering learning, progress and enjoyment in your life. (PS – after writing this, I went back the following week, and when our teacher said 'Well, let's make a start everyone', I swear someone said 'Do we have to?')

Sometimes people say 'I have to' because they're afraid it would be uncool to admit they enjoy something. Other times it's part of an excuse package such as 'I can't come with you because I have to go to the gym.' Sounds great but it still reinforces to your subconscious mind that the gym is a chore. Just say 'I can't come with you because I planned to go to the gym.'

Pay attention to any language you use that takes away your free will

I've heard clients say things like 'My personal trainer is making me do such and such.' No, you're choosing to let your personal trainer guide you. Why not fully enter into the spirit of that? An even worse example of this sort of language is to say things like, 'My kids are making me so angry.' No, you're choosing to be angry. It's *your* reaction to a particular event.

Also be very careful about saying 'I hate . . .' If you 'hate' vegetables, exercise, water (yes, I've heard this one) or whatever, it's the perfect excuse not to make them part of your life . . . except that it's not (the perfect excuse). You can find a way to eat vegetables, consume water and do an activity you enjoy. And you don't have to 'hate' traffic or other people. They might be 'challenging' or 'not your favourite thing', but whenever you speak of hate you're leaking energy big time. Have another look at the **Vitality Vessel** in **Chapter 4** to see what I mean.

Next, think about how you label yourself. Do you tell people what a dummy you are, how uncreative you are, or how terrible you are at maths? These labels often form part of our regular internal dialogues, and the more you say and think them, the more your subconscious mind believes and conforms to them. A wicked variation of this labelling is 'I've always been •••• (a worrier, clumsy, fat, hopeless at fixing things).' Not only does it label you, it absolves you of any responsibility to do anything about it because your subconscious mind completes the sentence with '. . . and always will be'. Try to replace this stuff with 'x is my challenge, and I'm improving', 'In the past I've had a tendency toward y, but I'm changing now.' You can also joke about your mistakes or weaker areas without criticising yourself. Just say 'oops, there's another lesson' (then define that lesson to yourself).

One last habit to consider, and that is – your answer to the question 'How are you?' Whatever you say is what you'll get more of, so choose carefully. Have a look at this chart, and think about your habitual answers:

A dose of my own medicine

As a result of changing *my* language (and beliefs) about tennis, I've gone from being utterly awful to being able to play in the village tennis tournament with my husband. I actually owe this little triumph completely to him because he used some of my own medicine on me. He's a good tennis player, and when I started talking about how terrible I was – binocular vision no good, not a natural sprinter (oh, yes, I had some brilliant excuses) – he insisted that I start saying, 'I'm a great tennis player, I just need some practice.' And we did practise – a lot. I'm not pretending that my skills improved simply through chanting some words, but they definitely helped me believe that I could actually hit the ball back over the net consistently. This boosted my learning when I did practise, and for me, made all the difference. Now I'm doing something healthy, sociable and spending quality time with my partner, all of which could have gone by the wayside if I had stuck with my limiting belief that I'm terrible at tennis.

Could you change this	**To this?**
Okay	Great
F.I.N.E. – Frazzled, Insecure, Neurotic and Exhausted	Super
Not so bad	Terrific
Surviving (survival is NOT ENOUGH)	Happy
Stressed out	Doing well
Exhausted	I'm winning
Knackered	Excited
Busy	Motivated

We'll look at this whole concept from a different angle in **Chapter 11 – Banish mental gremlins**, because the thoughts we choose have such an impact on energy levels.

Energy is contagious, positive or negative

Jeff was a memorable client of mine, mostly because of the vociferous colourfulness of his language when we first met. He was pretty stressed out, and he had no problems telling me *why* he was stressed out. 'I can't stand the traffic I face on the way to work. It's murder.' And he told me how he hated it when his colleagues promised things they couldn't, or didn't deliver. 'It just pisses me off so much', he said. His company had just been restructured, and he blamed this for making him unhappy. I thought: How in the world can I help this guy to turn his thinking around? So I challenged him to simply not say the words 'hate', 'can't stand' or 'pissed off' for three days straight. I said I'd phone him at the end of three days to find out what happened. Predictably, he said he hadn't done too well with his assignment. The first day, he didn't really notice those words in his statements and thoughts until a little while after he'd said them, if at all. On days two and three, he was beginning to notice, but only just after he'd blurted them out. What the exercise taught him, though, was that he could notice his language, and he had the potential to change it. He continued to work on it, and became aware of the effect this negativity had not only on him, but colleagues and family. Although we worked on quite a range of stress management measures, he said that consciously changing his language had the most positive effect on his life and his blood pressure. Is there an area of your life where you need to make a clear choice about your focus, in order to stop leaking energy like Jeff was? You are the only one who can do this.

Answer these questions as a way to help you start using language to your own energy advantage. You can download a clean copy from **www.stop-making-excuses.com**. If you find you're struggling with remembering when you use certain words, that's okay. Your assignment is to start paying more attention to your language so that you can choose it more proactively.

When do you say 'I can't'?

....

....

What will you replace it with?

....

....

What do you repeatedly say you 'should' do or that you'll 'try to do'?

....

....

What will you replace it with?

....

....

What do you say you 'have to' do?

✎ ....

....

What will you replace this with?

✎ ....

....

What do you say you 'hate'?

✎ ....

....

What will you replace this with?

Sounds like a broken record doesn't it? Well, that's the point.

✎ ....

....

How do you answer the question, 'How are you?'

✎ ....

....

If it isn't energising you, what could you answer instead?

✎ ....

....

Do you say that others 'make you' angry, sad, frustrated, demotivated?

✎ ....

....

How could you break this habit and take responsibility for your own emotions?

✎ ....

....

" *We cannot change anything until we accept it.* **"**

C. G. JUNG

" *Accept that some days you're the pigeon, and some days you're the statue.* **"**

RICKY GERVAIS

CHAPTER 8

Accepting what you have to give up to get what you want

Before you think I'm a killjoy for bringing up what you might have to give up in exchange for more energy, I ask you to read on with an open mind. Honestly, I'm all for enjoying life. I never tell people to subsist on lentils and wheatgrass juice. Most of us, including me, want some treats in life. We want good wine, luscious ice cream, or simply a long lie-in on a Sunday morning. All that's fine, as long as it's in small doses. I'm a big believer that a little of what you fancy does you good.

The point of this chapter is that there might be something that you must give up in order for you to have the vitality you want. You have three choices about this:

1. Don't give up that thing you love, but take the consequences
2. Do give up that thing, and feel resentful
3. Give up that thing and embrace that it is the price you pay to get what you want.

Could you just **accept** giving something up that you enjoy, but you know is detrimental to your vitality? We'd all like to pretend that if we are super-good in other areas, we won't have to give this thing up. Like if I work out extra hard then those cream cakes won't clog my arteries. Or skipping breakfast means I can have a chocolate bar in the afternoon. I've even had smokers tell me that they're probably okay because they work out every day, and doesn't that really clear your lungs out? Er, no.

> *Acceptance is not submission; it is acknowledgment of the facts of a situation. Then deciding what you're going to do about it.*
> KATHLEEN CASEY THEISEN, AMERICAN SOCIOLOGIST AND AUTHOR OF *EACH DAY A NEW BEGINNING: DAILY MEDITATIONS FOR WOMEN*

You can't beat Mother Nature, and if that second or third glass of wine in the evening makes you tired the next day, no amount of ginseng tea in the morning is going to give you the energy back. Only skipping the wine will do the trick.

What if your diet is great but you simply can't resist tortilla chips? You get through a giant bag of them every week (you know the ones that say 'share with friends'? Ha!), justifying that they *are* made of corn after all, and you eat them with low-fat salsa. Well, if you're trying to lose weight you might have to lose those chips.

On the subject of being overweight, do you know what Britain's fattest man says? 'I'd do anything to lose this weight.' Anything except not eat a double fry-up for breakfast, a triple helping of shepherd's pie for lunch, and an enormous curry for dinner. And did I mention the 20 pints of lager at the pub before dinner? Despite his current health woes (leg sores and breathing difficulties), this man is not yet accepting what he must give up in order to change. He does admit that he weighs 49 stone as a result of his own 'greed', but he is not at the point where he is prepared to give up anything in order to feel better.

Making time

Kerri is a busy working mother who came to me because she was stressed out and said that she felt 'shattered'. She was willing to change a range of things about her lifestyle to get some energy back but claimed she had no time to exercise. With two young ones of my own, I understood her challenge, but we started to talk through her daily routine to look for opportunities. It transpired that three nights a week she raced home from work to watch 'Eastenders'! I suggested she just give that up and go home via the gym instead. 'Oh, no I couldn't give up "Eastenders"', she said. Hello! Why is that more important than your health? With some prodding, she did see the lack of logic, and understood that she didn't really value soap operas above being healthy for the sake of her children. She made the swap. She lost 10 pounds over the next 6 months, and significantly decreased her stress levels, too. Kerri's story is a good example of how silly and trivial our excuses can be, yet hugely disempowering.

But my reasons are REAL

Think Kerri doesn't even know she's born? 'Time to watch "Eastenders"? Like I could ever do that!' I have conversations with clients all the time that carefully lay out every moment of the day filled with vital work and caring responsibilities, and only six hours of sleep a night. They then look at me defiantly as if to say, 'See! I truly have no time to exercise, prepare healthy food, build my relationships, or whatever.' What I say to them is that everyone has the same 24 hours in a day, and how you fill it is your choice. If you want to feel good (and continue to feel good as you age), you might have to make some choices that involve reducing your work commitments, and increasing your commitment to yourself.

Here's a worksheet to help you accept losing something you enjoy, and move on to habits that serve you better. You can download a clean copy from **www.stop-making-excuses.com**.

What do you need to simply accept what has to change in your life for you to be as energetic, slim, fit, focussed or creative as you'd like?

Examples: giving up your addiction to surfing the net or computer games late at night; reducing your alcohol, caffeine, chocolate, doughnut, crisp consumption; reducing your commitments; reducing your television time; giving up your need for control.

✎ ....

....

....

If you gave this thing up, or drastically reduced it, what benefits would that bring?

Be very specific and detailed in your answer. 'I'd feel better' is not going to motivate you enough.

✎ ....

....

....

Now write down a reason you're happy to stop this behaviour/habit/ addiction – a statement that puts the loss in a completely positive light.

For example: Giving up coffee during my working day means that I'll be less stressed and more focussed. I'll sleep better and have more energy.

✎ ....

....

....

Excellent. Now, just like in Chapter 6, write this final statement out in big, bold letters and put it somewhere you'll see it every single day, for at least three weeks. If you keep this statement in your head as well, and say it to yourself every time you feel the temptation, you'll begin to associate *positive feelings* with *not* doing the habit. Do it now because if you don't, the moment of motivation to take this step will evaporate.

I hope that this chapter has swept up more of your poor energy habits and excuses. Now that you've begun to 'Stop Making Excuses', you're ready to 'Start Living with Energy'. **Part III – Vitality Now!** is full of information, practical tips and tools for creating your life full of energy and vigour!

Vitality now! 15 essential energy strategies

> **"** *Where there is no vision, the people perish.* **"**
> PROVERBS 29:18

> **"** *The moment the vision goes it's over.* **"**
> ROGER BLACK, OLYMPIC 400m MEDALLIST

CHAPTER 9

What is vitality for you?

When you hear the word 'vitality', does it conjure up images of happy, smiling people cycling on a sunny day? A windsurfer storming through the waves, or someone meditating under a tree?

Does it seem those happy, smiling people could never be you? Whatever you think, you DO have the potential to live a life of vitality. This section of the book, **Vitality Now!** is all about strategies to get you there.

The Chambers dictionary defines vitality as 'the quality of being fully or intensely alive; the capacity to endure and flourish'. And for most people, it is about an enduring energy, not one big flash that burns out quickly.

I've asked over one thousand workshop delegates to define vitality, and this is a list of words that consistently come up:

Energy

Life/Living

Wellbeing

Health

Fun

Love

Light

Serenity

One delegate said 'it is a feeling of lightness of being, of feeling you have the energy to do anything you want to go for.'

I think that vitality is about all **FOUR ENERGIES** (see Chapter 3) and includes stamina, love, mental sharpness, spark and sense of purpose. The most important thing, of course, is how *you* define it, what it feels and looks like for *you*.

Try the following short worksheet to help you clarify and visualise what you are going for when you say you want more vitality. You can print out a clean copy at **www.stop-making-excuses.com**.

If you could only use one word to define vitality, what would it be? (It can be something funky like Vavoom or Zing, if you like)

✎ ....

....

When you have vitality, what does it feel like?

✎ ....

....

When you have vitality, what do you look like?

✎ ....

....

When you have vitality, what personal qualities do you display?

For example, more patience, creativity or leadership.

✎ ....

....

What short, memorable definition of vitality could you construct for yourself that will help you get there (or stay there)?

For example: Power Up, Full-On Energy, Verve & Nerve, Go For It, Just Do It, The Full Monty.

✎ ....

....

Go back to **Chapter 1** and look again at 'What You Want'. Combine it with these images and feelings about vitality, and you've got a fabulous picture of you at your best, reaching your full potential. Visualising the vitality, energy, life and health you want is a critical part of getting there – and that's exactly what we're going to do in the next chapter.

Throughout this central portion of the book (Chapters 10–24) we'll cover a whole range of methods for generating more vitality and energy, from mental to physical to emotional – *and* have a look at how to have more passion and spirit!

Maybe you just need to refocus . . .

Many people have terrific energy habits that have lapsed, or have bits and pieces in place that don't add up to a joined-up strategy for health and vitality. You might only need to refocus your attention onto why this is important and what you need to do.

A lovely friend of mine who had breast cancer told me that it re-focussed her attention on what was really important in life, and how she wants to spend her time. 'Until you face something like that, you don't face your own mortality.'

I asked her specifically about energy habits, and she definitely does have some new ones: fresh juice every morning, no more milk, and she takes spirulina [a supplement thought to be a 'superfood' because it is high in both antioxidants and essential fatty acids]. She used to go to the gym, but goes more religiously now.

She says she has a 'renewed state of mind' as a result of her experience of a potentially life-threatening disease. She's more laid back about life, though she says she's less tolerant of people who moan about small things.

Are you too focussed on the insignificant things to look after your own vitality?

MENTAL
ENERGY

Of the **FOUR ENERGIES**, I'm starting with **MENTAL ENERGY** because this book is about getting your head into a different space – a place where you strive for energy and for feeling good as a no-debate, no-brainer. The following five chapters, 10–14, are about the key mental skills you need to have more brain horsepower and more success in creating the life you want: *a life with fabulous energy*.

" *Whatever the mind can conceive and believe, it can achieve.* "

NAPOLEON HILL, AUTHOR OF *THINK AND GROW RICH*

" *I believe in luck: how else can you explain the success of those you dislike?* "

JEAN COCTEAU, FRENCH POET AND NOVELIST

CHAPTER 10

Visualise to energise

The single most important thing you can do to stop making excuses and start living with energy is to **VISUALISE** it. If you can create a healthy, vibrant and joyous state in your mind (whether you see it, hear it or feel it), you are half way there. Visualising has a certain magic quality about it because it puts you continually in the right frame of mind to take the actions that will bring results. It brings confidence to your tone of voice and body language that others can read, even if only subliminally. You are literally using the power of your mind to create the life you want.

Most top athletes know the value of this and make it an essential part of their training. Tiger Woods says that 'Visualization has become a major part of my shotmaking . . .'. Gold medal-winning triathlete Brigitte McMahon said that she visualised her sprint to the finish many times before arriving in Sydney – that she had 'planned the outcome of the race'. Successful people all over the world use this as a part of their daily routine, and you can too. Oprah Winfrey says that, 'I do believe, and I have seen in my own life, that creative visualization works.'

It's so simple. The thing is, **you must make the time to do it**. If it's not scheduled into your day or something you do habitually at a certain time, for instance, on waking, it's pretty unlikely it will happen. In my own life, visualising what I want has brought astonishing results: a contract with a dream client, a publishing deal for this book and an opportunity to go horse riding on a regular basis – to name but a few. Since I started using this technique five years ago, I began to see a clear pattern. When I used visualisation, it brought results, and when I didn't, I didn't seem to have the same success. So as you can imagine, I'm using it pretty regularly now.

Live with energy

Tracks 1–4 on the Live with Energy CD included with this book are guided visualisations to help you achieve any change you want to make. Each one begins with a relaxation sequence because it makes the visualisations more effective. When you get into a relaxed state, your subconscious mind is more open to suggestion (which, by the way, is how hypnotism works).

The more frequently you do the same visualisation the more fervently your subconscious mind will believe it, and begin to act in accordance with it. The subconscious mind is actually pretty gullible, and will believe anything it's told repeatedly. This is why children who are told they are stupid actually become so, and children who are told they are gifted often begin to excel academically. Think about why Muhammad Ali kept saying 'I am the greatest'. He was creating it and believing it over and over in his head – and you don't get to be heavyweight champion of the world three times if you're harbouring self-doubt!

The best thing, of course, is to experience the power of visualisation for yourself. I urge you to do at least one visualisation per day that is about your energy, health, vitality, desired new habits or any outcome you're hoping for, be it a promotion or a fabulous partner. I'm not saying that if you're 5'5" you can visualise your way to becoming a professional basketball player. I am saying that you should not be held back by limiting beliefs, worries, tendency to procrastinate or rationalise, or by previous achievement. Try this powerful method for energy and goal achievement wholeheartedly, and you will not be disappointed.

Remember that although I'm using the word 'visualising', I'm actually talking about creating the experience of something in your mind, whether it's pictures, sounds or feelings. Some people are better at conjuring up what it would feel like to have unlimited energy than what it would look like. When you listen to the CD, you'll notice that I'm careful to enable any sort of imagining that takes you to your desired place, by encouraging visual, audible and kinaesthetic (feeling) experience.

Dream boards

Another fantastic tool for visualising what you want is a **_Dream Board_**. Using any size wooden board or poster board, you pin or glue on the pictures of what you want your life to look like, put it in a prominent place, and study it two or three times a day – for instance, on waking, and before turning out the light at night. That's why I keep mine right by my bed. But some of my clients have put them on refrigerators (we're talking paper posters here), in cars, or by bathroom mirrors. One client even taped a picture of Maria Sharapova to her tennis racquet cover, and she swears it has made her play better.

I highly recommend trying a dream board to help you reach your energy goals. For example, if your goal is to lose weight, you could dig out a picture of slim you, or use a picture of your face stuck on Angelina Jolie's body! If you're trying to get in physical shape, add some pictures of happy, smiling people looking energised and fit. If you want a happier family, use happy family pictures.

And you don't have to stop there. Put on your dream board your dream house, boat, car, holiday, or a total in a savings account. I have all of that on mine, AND I have a picture of THIS book right beside _The_

Sunday Times Bestseller list. THAT gets me energised more than anything else right now, because I'm so passionate and excited about helping people to feel better than they ever have. It's a daily shot of megawatt energy to look at that part of my dream board. But it's not *only* a source of energy. Visualising those things will lead me there, and they can lead you, too.

All I ask of you at the close of this chapter is to take at least **one** action around creating the outcomes you want in your head. If you choose not to, think about why. Does it seem like too much hard work? If you can't even take one action toward this, how are you going to bust your long-standing excuses? Don't think it will work? Why not try it consistently for three to six weeks? Adding some of this stuff to your life is fun and enhances creativity. You've got nothing to lose and everything to gain.

> *Men are not disturbed by things, but the view they take of things.*

EPICTETUS (55–135 A.D.)

> *What about things like bullets?*

HERB KIMMEL, BEHAVIOURALIST, PROFESSOR OF PSYCHOLOGY, UPON HEARING THE ABOVE QUOTE

CHAPTER 11

Banish mental gremlins

The last chapter was all about creating powerful visualisations of your energy and vitality, but there's something that can stomp on positive visualisations and thoughts, and even kill them: ***limiting beliefs***. Limiting beliefs are fears and ego-driven negative thoughts I call **MENTAL GREMLINS**. These little beasts reside in your mind, revealing themselves just when they can blow your confidence, add pressure to your project, or just generally ruin your day.

Maybe you've never noticed your own self-chatter – little voices inside your head that chat to you. They remind you of things, sometimes encourage you (these are the mental good fairies), but too often they criticise you or tell you that you mustn't fail, that change will be very bad, or some such rubbish.

Here are some examples of common mental gremlins:

- Everything has to be perfect
- I have to be right
- I have to have control
- I have to be strong
- I'm afraid of . . . rejection, failure, change
- I can't change
- Nothing ever works
- This isn't fair
- I can't handle this
- I can't ask for help
- I must . . . I should . . . I ought
- Hurry up
- I'm so clumsy
- I'm such an idiot
- I'll never be able to . . .
- I'll never be a success at . . .

Recognise any of these? You probably do, and you might have some gems of your own. After your excuses, they are your *biggest* barrier to achieving the energy, vitality, happiness and great life that you want.

But you know what? YOU DON'T HAVE TO PUT UP WITH THEM ANYMORE! You have the power to bounce them right out of your mind. In order to do this, *first* you must **believe** that you have the power, and *second* you must **be persistent** in your efforts to eradicate them. Let's take a look at how you'd achieve these two things.

Belief

Your belief that you can banish mental gremlins is critical to your success. Sadly, most people think they are stuck with these monsters, and this in itself becomes a great excuse for bad energy habits. Statements such as 'I can't help it, I'm a worrier' or 'I'm just a perfectionist and I guess I'll never change' are clear examples. As I said in **Chapter**

7 – Mind your language, you must be very careful about the things you tell yourself repeatedly. You'll believe them.

Remember that your mind is completely under your control. That's an obvious, common sense statement, but not believed or utilised by everyone. Using the power you have to control your own mind makes you the master of your own destiny, and it's truly awesome. Don't waste this power. As soon as you believe this power is yours, it will no longer be in the Gremlins' clutches.

If you need further confidence in your ability to dominate your mental gremlins, ask yourself: 'Who is actually saying these things to me?' If the answer comes back: my father, mother, brother, sister, school bully, teacher or similar, then you must say out loud to these people: 'You do not have any control or power over me. You never really did. The only control you have is what I give you. Every time I hear you I am going to boot you straight out of my head and refocus on something positive' (you can use an affirming statement that you'll develop in Chapter 13 ☺).

If your answer to 'who is saying these things?' is 'I don't know', you can say something like, 'You are just a pathetic gremlin, and what you're saying is a load of rubbish' . . . then continue with your affirming statement.

If you're still not convinced of your power to do this, consider this amazing quote by Viktor Frankl. It is one of the most empowering statements I have ever read. He said:

'. . . everything can be taken from a man but one thing: the last of human freedoms – to choose one's attitude in any given set of circumstances.'

When he wrote this, he really meant *any* circumstances. Viktor Frankl was an Austrian psychologist who was imprisoned in four different Nazi concentration camps during World War II. He said that the times when things looked bleakest were the times he forced the despair out of his head by focussing on happy memories from the past and hopes of his life *when* he got out – not 'if'. He understood the power of the mind to choose thoughts that would help him to survive, not spiral him down even further. In his case, it really was a matter of life or death.

Persistence

So if you now believe that you *do* have the power to choose your thoughts, how are you going to exterminate the gremlins for good? Well, it's probably a life's work. But there's no reason not to start now and pick them off one by one.

You know how when you learn something new, the process is slow the first few times you use this knowledge, but speeds up over time? The required thought patterns or actions eventually become second nature or automatic. In the same way, getting rid of the gremlins and replacing them with more useful thoughts will take time – but can become second nature. This is where the **persistence** comes in. Let's look at the tools you can use and how you can maintain your attack on any thoughts that bring you down.

❝ *Stand guard at the door of your mind.* ❞
ANTHONY ROBBINS

First off, when you recognise a gremlin and decide to exterminate it, summon up a memory that challenges and counteracts it. For instance, instead of thinking 'I can't handle this', you can recall a time you've handled things competently, coolly and calmly. Be prepared with a number of examples to deliberately focus on when your confidence wobbles. To add to the staying power of this idea, make a note of these memories and put them in your diary.

> " We create our lives a thought at a time. And sometimes, it comes down to changing a thought such as 'Why did this happen to me?' into 'There is a divine plan and there is a reason for this, and my choice is to create the most positive reaction I can. "
> DEE WALLACE STONE

Another simple tool you can use to change your thoughts is to distract yourself with thoughts of an upcoming fun event, by phoning a friend, or doing some light reading. You can also work on a project that takes all your attention and mental effort, or by solving some sort of puzzle. This is a tactic that works well if you are a worrier, because you can't stay in that worry loop when you're thoroughly absorbed in something else. Some people in high-pressure jobs switch off by doing dangerous sports such as rock climbing or downhill mountain biking because it requires 100% focus on the activity, and it's like being in another world. The way to infuse your life with this sort of habit is to have the sudoku book handy, or make a date to do that sporty activity with a group.

A third, and one of the most effective ways to beat the gremlins is to choose a more empowering statement to focus on and repeat to yourself or out loud. For example, you might decide to think, 'I can do this' and deliberately refocus your mind on this statement whenever the 'I can't handle this' gremlin rears its ugly head. **Chapter 13 – Affirmations and celebrations** is all about these 'affirmational' statements and how to make them stick.

Don't wait until you 'have time' for this because it will never materialise. Make it 'up front and present' in your life in whatever way you need to – in your handbag, briefcase, car, on the table by the front door, as a string around your finger reminder, your mobile phone greeting – be creative!

The power of focus

When Richard Branson and Per Lindstrand made their record-breaking hot-air balloon crossing of the Pacific Ocean, lost fuel tanks, fire and uncontrollable increases in altitude threatened not only the journey but their lives. It would have been easy to spiral into: 'Oh my God we're doomed, we're going to die.' But Richard used the tools of distraction and focus astonishingly well. He says in his auto-biography *Losing My Virginity*:

'I put all thoughts of death out of my head, and for the next ten hours concentrated intently on the dials . . . I just looked at the dials and pretended that I was driving some sort of weightless car which I had to keep within a ribbon of road.'

He also focussed on speaking to the video camera, pretending he was speaking to his family and that all was well. If it can be done in life-threatening crises, then you can easily use this tool in everyday life to maintain focus on what you want instead of on self-imposed limitations.

Answer these questions here, or download a clean copy from **www.stop-making-excuses.com**.

What are your top three mental gremlins?

If you don't know, don't worry. Just pay attention to the voices in your head over the next week or so, and start to be aware of any messages that bring you down.

✎ ....

....

How will you 'challenge' these gremlins – that is, increase your belief that they're stupid and false?

✎ ....

....

What tools will you use when they show up in your head, and how will you use them? Be specific!

✎ ....

....

" *Never limit yourself because of others'*
limited imagination; never limit others
because of your own limited imagination. **"**

MAE JEMISON, ASTRONAUT

" *Too bad all the people who know how to*
run the country are busy driving
taxi cabs and cutting hair. **"**

ANONYMOUS

CHAPTER 12

Get in control!

Now that you understand about the destructiveness of mental gremlins, and perhaps have a greater awareness of them in yourself, I want to look at the specific sort of gremlin that is particularly energy-draining. It's the one that urges us to stay in control of everything. Vague voices give us reasons we ought to be in charge, or why things ought to be done our way. It stops us from listening, learning and creating collaborative relationships.

It's funny that some people spend so much energy seeking to control other people and events, when in fact the only thing we have total control over is ourselves. It's a common issue, certainly among my clients, most of whom are high achievers. They like the feeling of being on top of everything, knowing what's going on and influencing decisions. There's no problem with that, except that they tend to confuse influence with control.

Influence vs control

> *Everything I do and say with anyone makes a difference.*
> GITA BELLIN

If we consciously try to influence something, we have the opportunity to develop a strategy. 'What does the decision-maker want?' 'What would motivate my subordinate to work hard on my project?' We tend to ask the right questions to influence effectively.

When we unconsciously try to be in control of others' work, behaviour or personality, we don't usually ask those questions. We attempt to take command through a louder voice, threats, passive-aggressive behaviour, disapproval, criticism, or emotional games like imposing guilt or withholding communication. This is an enormous emotional and mental drain, and even if it seems to work in the short term, it almost never works in the long term because it is not about real relationship building. In short, it wears you out.

When we influence people, and everyone wins (i.e. they win and we win), the relationship is strengthened. When we bully, cajole or create such a fuss others give in, the relationship is weakened. Eventually, there is no relationship at all.

Getting buy-in

Have you ever had a team member who you could count on for the negative comment? 'We tried that and it didn't work.' 'Are you kidding? Ops will never agree to that.' 'I can't believe they expect us to do that! It's so unfair. Don't you guys agree?' I worked with a team in a consultancy firm where this was exactly the case. The woman in question, Lisa, was not actually a bad person, she just had a habit of negativity, and it was bringing everyone down. The manager of this team thought everyone was stressed out, but that wasn't the problem at all. They were **unmotivated** for a number of reasons, one was being so tired of this persistent negativity. I needed to help the team find some motivation, and also to influence this woman's behaviour without blaming or controlling her, which would surely only make her worse.

I spent a day with the team helping them, amongst other things, to formulate a set of principles by which they would all agree to work. It was critical to get everyone's buy-in to this, because when people feel ownership of ideas, they will be influenced by them. The team chose as their guiding principles: asking for help, innovation, honesty, respect, positivity and customer delight.

A few weeks later I spoke to the team manager to see how things were going. She had been able to quote the team agreement back to the negative woman by saying, 'Lisa, thanks very much for that. Do you remember our team values? Can you find a way of rephrasing that so it's positive?' She did it in a semi-joking way, so Lisa didn't lose face, and had actually got a positive response.

Can you think of a situation in your life where you could get a team, colleague, family or partner to agree to operate by a certain set of principles to save you constantly being frustrated by their behaviour? When you have these 'brave conversations', you may find that you have a much greater understanding of them, they have a better understanding of you, and your energy is freed up for much better things.

Think of conversations you've had with family members, colleagues, bosses or shop staff. Analyse how much you've influenced positively, and how much you've sought to control things. I'm asking you to be honest about your need for control, and contemplate where you could let go of it saving oodles of energy.

Answer these questions here, or download a clean copy from **www.stop-making-excuses.com**.

What areas of your life do you try to control rather than positively influence?

For example, children, partner, colleagues, a project, housework.

✍ ....

....

....

Describe what happens to your energy levels when you (inevitably) fail to keep control of these things?

✍ ....

....

....

Brainstorm here about how you could positively influence these areas rather than try to get control:

✍ ....

....

....

Of those ideas, what one thing will you commit to doing?

✍ ....

....

....

How will you review whether you've succeeded in making this change?

✎ ....

....

....

It's the repetition of affirmations that leads to belief. And once that belief becomes a deep conviction, things begin to happen.

CLAUDE M. BRISTOL, AUTHOR OF BESTSELLER
THE MAGIC OF BELIEVING

I guess I just prefer to see the dark side of things. The glass is always half empty. And cracked. And I just cut my lip on it. And chipped a tooth.

JANEANE GAROFALO, COMEDIAN, ACTRESS AND
CO-HOST OF AMERICAN RADIO'S 'THE MAJORITY REPORT'

CHAPTER 13

Affirmations and celebrations

D id you ever have the experience of basking in the glow of an achievement, or a sincere compliment from someone you love and respect? And in that moment, you felt that you were beaming energy? We've all been there at some point. Now imagine creating that feeling for yourself, every single day. It is so simple, it's child's play. And young children are indeed good at this. When they paint a picture, they know it's a masterpiece, and when they build a fort, they're king or queen of the castle. This is because they don't have so many gremlins yet, and they're not yet comparing themselves to the rest of the world.

We can learn to be more like that again! We can tell ourselves we're awesome, and celebrate our successes. I call these fun and powerful tools **affirmations** and **celebrations**, and we can use them for ourselves and for loved ones.

Affirmations

Affirmations are statements we make either in our heads or out loud that will improve our emotions, attitudes, self-belief and sense of purpose. They're a huge mental and emotional energy boost! You can use affirmations in a number of ways:

- At the beginning of each day to choose how you feel or to count your blessings
- To challenge negative thoughts (mental gremlins) and emotions
- To challenge your excuses
- Just before a meeting, presentation or tricky conversation where you want to be you at your best
- In situations where you want to display a certain quality
- At the end of each day to re-affirm what you've accomplished, and what you've learned.

In the last two chapters you've had a chance to think about the sorts of mental and emotional energy drainers you possess, and now it's time to re-write your script. I urge you to surround yourself with messages that will help you to feel energised, successful and just generally fantastic. Put them up by your bathroom mirror, on your refrigerator, in your car, use them as screen savers and leave notes to yourself in desk drawers. You can do this for your spouse and children, too!

Whatever message you choose for yourself, saturate yourself with it for at least 21 days – seeing it and saying it at least three times every one of these days. It takes at least this long to become embedded in your subconscious mind. You'll know when it's embedded because it will become an automatic thought. When it's an automatic thought process, you'll start behaving in ways that will lead you to your goal, to display this trait, or to this way of being/feeling.

It's not rocket science, but not very many people use this magic trick for creating the life they want. Either they're sceptical (but haven't tried

it, or swear they've chanted 'I've won the lottery' for three months and it didn't work), 'don't have time', or just don't know about this easy way to re-programme their thoughts. *But*, I've had disbelieving clients come back to me with tales of increased calmness, confidence and even income as a result of using affirmations. So don't knock it till you've tried it.

My recommendation is that you devise at least one clever, funny, memorable affirmation that will stick with you like a record you hear on the radio. Here is a whole range of affirmations (all created by my clients for themselves) from the simple to the outrageous. Feel free to borrow from this list when you create your own:

- I am calm
- I am capable
- I'm awesome!
- I'm too blessed to be stressed
- I solve problems
- I choose my reaction
- I choose to be happy
- I find the right people at the right time
- I make it happen
- Damn I'm good
- I've got the power!
- I am living my vision of success
- I can negotiate

- I am creative
- I prosper wherever I turn
- Life is what I'm making it
- Breathe more, smile more, laugh more, live more
- This is my best decade
- I can change the now.

You'll notice that all of the above affirmations are positive (i.e. no negative words) and in the present tense, which sends a straightforward message to your subconscious mind – I *am* doing this or feeling this *now*. It's happening NOW.

Some of my clients, however, have found that the following affirmations have helped them hugely, because these statements counteracted their own personal gremlins (perfectionism, people-pleasing, controlling, being too timid)

- You can't please everyone
- Things don't have to be perfect
- I can't control everything / Let go of control!
- Move over, Madonna!

Still another type of affirmational statement is an inspirational quotation that speaks to you in your current situation. Some of them might seem negative, but can still have a powerful, motivating effect.

- To succeed in business, be daring, be first, be different
- What doesn't kill you makes you stronger
- He who angers you conquers you
- At lowest ebb the tide always turns
- I don't know the key to success, but the key to failure is trying to please everyone – Bill Cosby
- I have learnt more from my failures than from my successes – Richard Branson
- No one can make you feel inferior without your consent – Eleanor Roosevelt

- We learn courageous action by going forward whenever fear urges us back – David Seabury
- Begin with the end in mind – Stephen Covey
- Determine that the thing can and shall be done, and then we shall find the way – Abraham Lincoln

If you want to see my entire collection of inspirational quotations, go to **www.stop-making-excuses.com** where you can download the document. Whatever affirmation you create for yourself, the key is to surround yourself with it and *believe it*.

You think you have challenges?

Linda, now aged 55, 'always had lots of illness'. Born just after World War II, her mother had toxaemia (blood poisoning), so she was small and jaundiced. Her immune system and energy were low right from the beginning of her life. She began having migraines at age 10. After that came severe bouts of depression, glandular fever and pneumonia. She had so many infections she became allergic to penicillin. From age 15 she was on tranquillisers and anti-depressants. But, as she put it, her family had a strong work ethic – you 'carry on and don't give up' – so that's what she did.

Then in 1999, Linda stopped functioning. She couldn't speak, write, read or hear properly. A psychiatrist diagnosed repetitive depressive neurosis, and she underwent therapy for six years. This therapy taught Linda how to process information differently in her brain – she said it was as if she had no search engine, and this was putting one in place. She learned that she had dysfunctional beliefs and that there was a mismatch between her high intellect and her low energy.

She was on the road to a new life with a new outlook when she was diagnosed with cancer in 2005. Sometimes life seems utterly unfair, but Linda told me that having cancer put in place the final bit of the jigsaw that made her rethink her life. 'I had to put into practice all that I'd learned. When I got cancer my whole outlook changed. I took ownership of what was happening to me and started to do something about it. No more victim. I also never lost my sense of humour. This was so important.'

To treat her cancer, Linda had two operations, chemotherapy and radiotherapy – the works. But she has been cancer free for over a year, and her energy and stamina are building all the time. She eats more healthily now – no more chocolate and biscuit addictions. And she listens to what her body needs, something she never did before.

She's certain that an optimistic attitude helped her to heal. She says, 'It's one thing to say "be positive" but you have to really feel it.'

Celebrations

"What we can or cannot do, what we consider possible or impossible, is rarely a function of our true capability. It is more likely a function of our beliefs about who we are."
ANTHONY ROBBINS

If you want more energy, make it a habit to **celebrate** your successes and accomplishments every day. This is **not** vanity. It's just another way of affirming to yourself that you're capable, talented and special. Very few of us have a constant cheerleader/fan/mentor to give us this sort of message, so we can do it for ourselves! Usually, in all our busy-ness, we finish one project and rush straight into the next one without even pausing for breath, let alone a review of what went well, how we dealt well with that client or wrote the report creatively. Put this practice in your life, and you'll not only feel more successful and satisfied with your achievements, you really *will* be, because your winning behaviours will be reinforced.

"Celebrate what you want to see more of."
THOMAS J. PETERS

Here are some questions you can ask yourself as a way to cultivate the habit of celebrations:

- To set you up at the start of the day, 'What challenges might I face today and how am I going to solve them creatively and assertively?'
- After a tricky phone call or sales call, 'What did I do well there? Was I well-prepared, charming, creative, persuasive? How did I do that?'
- When you finish a big task, pat yourself on the back, say 'well done' and think about how you used your skills and strengths to good advantage
- At the end of each day, 'What went well today?', 'What was the best part of my day today and why?'

You can use any of these celebration tools with your kids or partner, too. It will strengthen their confidence and your relationship, too.

Analysing success

There's a story about an international rugby team that turned around their losing streak by learning to celebrate success in a new way. The losing coach was sacked, and when the new coach took over, he noticed that when the team lost, they spent a lot of time going over game footage and analysing what had gone wrong. He asked the team, 'What do you do when you win?' 'That's easy', they said, 'we go to the pub!'

So one change this coach made was to bring the team together to analyse their formulas for success. This helped the team to have a more positive focus when playing. Their thought processes were more about the things they needed to do to be successful rather than what to avoid doing in order not to lose!

Stephen Covey, in his bestseller *The Seven Habits of Highly Effective People* reminds readers that 'We go toward what we focus on'. In order to make a behaviour change, it is far easier to work *toward* the desired behaviour (that we have clearly defined and visualised) than to *refrain* from the unwanted behaviour. It's effective not only for sporting success, but for things like smoking cessation, dieting, fitness and developing any positive trait you want.

Now for the really fun part.

Answer these questions here or download a clean copy from **www.stop-making-excuses.com**.

What are some affirmational statements that you can create to help you to overcome excuses, negative thought patterns, and to have the personal traits and life *you* want? You can write as many as you like, but I suggest between one and three.

✎..

....

....

Next you can make colourful, artistic posters with your affirmations on them. Really go for it with coloured pens, stickers and glitter glue! Be a kid again. This might sound silly, and you might be tempted to skip this step, but it's important for three reasons:

1. When you create a poster like this, it helps to cement the affirmation into your head

2. Doing art like this is a great way to shift mental gears, and open up your creativity in other areas

3. It's fun! I make nearly every workshop group do this exercise, and I *always* have trouble getting them to stop playing!

Now go and hang the posters where you'll see them every day, preferably at least three times.

What are several ways you can celebrate your successes more often and more memorably?

✎..

....

....

How will you remind yourself to do this enough times to make it a habit?

✍ ....

....

....

Creativity often consists of merely turning up what is already there. Did you know that right and left shoes were thought up only a little over a century ago?

BERNICE FITZ-GIBBON (1894–1982), PIONEER IN RETAIL ADVERTISING

The secret of creativity is knowing how to hide your sources.

ALBERT EINSTEIN

CHAPTER 14

Get creative

We've now had four chapters about how to increase mental energy that will also help you to bust your excuses and start living with more energy: visualising, feeling in control, exterminating gremlins and creating a positive mindset. There's another way you can increase mental energy that will, again, help you to get rid of your excuses forever – it's your *personal creativity*. Creativity is about looking at things in a new way so that you can get away from your old patterns, and that's the essence of this book.

First off, you absolutely CANNOT say at this point, 'Oh, I'm not creative.' If that's your mantra, go back to the last chapter and make your affirmation, 'I am creative!' Everyone has creativity in them. Maybe you just don't tap into yours very often.

If you keep developing your creativity throughout your life, you'll be better equipped to organise your busy, complex life in a way that still gives you satisfaction, joy and the space to look after yourself properly. You'll also be better at problem-solving and meeting challenges. In my experience, it's when the big challenges arise that people tend to completely disregard their own health and energy needs.

So, how are you going to get creative? I've read a number of books and articles about how to increase creativity, and although their messages have been worthy, I feel they've been over-complicated. Quite frankly, a number of them bored me stiff. I think that the most important thing you must do in order to be creative is to develop a belief that *everyone* has a creative nature within him or her. The particular gifts and talents people have are different, of course, but you have the capacity to be wonderfully creative. It's just that this aspect of you may have lain dormant since childhood through a lack of practice and a lack of belief that you can have flair and style, great new ideas and innovative solutions.

I spent years telling myself that I wasn't creative. I was a *scientist*, for goodness sake, and I had this idea that I was great at research, and also good at explaining complex ideas to people. But my own ideas? Nah! Then I started running workshops on stress and health management, and I found it wasn't enough just to help people understand stuff. If I was going to move them to change their ways and their lives, I needed to find creative ways to enthuse, motivate, cajole and excite them – to get them to remember that they could feel great. One day I was writing a new workshop, and I kept asking myself the question, 'How can I make these concepts stick for my delegates?' I kept getting the half answer: I'm going to have to be creative. And it just hit me . . . *I have to be creative.* I decided in that moment that, OK, I *am* creative. Since then, every project I begin, I begin knowing that I'm going to come up with some cool ideas, and I haven't looked back.

LIVE WITH ENERGY PIN-UP

Below are 10 practical ways that you can make the shift into greater creativity. Get practising, and start reaping the energy that comes from creative flow. This pin-up list can be printed from the website **www. stop-making-excuses.com**.

1. Set aside some quality time to allow yourself to think creatively. This is essential, because when you are on the treadmill of your day, you are task-oriented, busy and often under time pressure. This is NOT conducive to creativity, as you're probably aware. You've got to diarise this or it won't happen.

2. Do some sort of creative process on a regular basis – at least once a week. This can be absolutely anything from sketching, to making music, to creating a scrapbook.

3. When faced with a challenge or any design project, pretend that you are the most creative designer in the world. What would you do then?

4. Another good pretend game is to imagine you are looking at the issue the way different professions would. What would a plumber make of this? What about a lawyer, a doctor, a General?

5. Spend some time in nature. Old forests, beaches, hills and fields have special energy that will charge up your creativity.

6. Use 'spider-grams' to generate new thoughts and ideas. Start with your central theme or challenge and write this in the centre of a blank sheet of paper. Circle it. Now begin to draw lines radiating out from this centre, each one attached to a related theme, or potential solution. Then each of these can have it's own web of ideas or solutions. Don't rule out anything, and keep going until you feel it's complete. This method can also clarify a current project and act as a to-do list.

7. Remember to brainstorm with other people. Bring your team, or a selected group together, clarify what you're brainstorming about, then start throwing ideas into the ring. You can also use the spider-gram system for group brainstorming.

8. Change your physiology, because this is critical when you're trying to be creative. Sit up, or stand up straight, lift your breastbone, roll your shoulders back and down, breathe from your belly, and let go of tension, particularly from your back, jaw and around your eyes. Another great way to let go of tension is to get some exercise.

Creativity is allowing yourself to make mistakes. Art is knowing which ones to keep.
SCOTT ADAMS

Never tell people how to do things. Tell them what to do and they will surprise you with their ingenuity.
GENERAL GEORGE SMITH PATTON, JR.

9. Do something to improve your brain chemistry. Smile (big) and laugh. Put on some music and dance and sing! No one's watching, honest!

10. When you're stuck, walk a figure of eight over and over, breathing calmly. Try it, it works!

You can probably guess what I'm going to ask you now. Answer these two simple questions here or download a clean copy from **www.stop-making-excuses.com**.

How will you enhance *your* creativity? Any of the above ideas or your own?

✍ ....

....

How will you make this a permanent habit?

✍ ....

....

PHYSICAL ENERGY

I took it easy on you by putting the chapters about mental energy first. Now let's get down to the serious business of how you look after yourself *physically*. Chapters 15–18 cover exercise, eating habits, sleep and relaxation. They really are a foundation for the other energies: imagine being sleep deprived, tense, hungry or completely out of shape. How's your resilience then? Plus, when you have limited physical energy, you're more than twice as likely to:

a) wallow in your excuses and
b) practise even worse habits in other areas of your life.

So go into this section ready to rethink how you live day to day, if you want to have more energy. The good news is that small changes to your physical habits can bring amazing energy revenues.

" *A vigorous five mile walk will do more good for an unhappy, but otherwise healthy adult than all the medicine and psychology in the world.* "

PAUL DUDLEY WHITE (1886–1973), AMERICAN CARDIOLOGIST, PIONEER IN PREVENTATIVE LIFESTYLE HABITS

" *I don't exercise. If God wanted me to bend over, he'd have put diamonds on the floor.* "

JOAN RIVERS

CHAPTER 15

Exit sloth, enter fox

Q uestion: Have you ever seen a fat fox? I've only ever seen one, in central London, walking between Italian restaurant dustbins. In the countryside, they are always jogging along, looking very lean and lithe. It's a way of life for them to be swiftly on the move. They cover a lot of ground (as opposed to say, sheep), and all that activity keeps them thin and fit. It's the same for us. To stay fit, slim and full of energy, we need to be moving around a lot, too.

The awesome benefits of exercise

The way our bodies and brains are wired, we think and feel best when we are active every day. Most of us have experienced the increases in stamina, strength and energy when we exercise. But exercise does more than just tone muscles and keep your heart healthy. It also improves mood and mental capacity by:

* Increasing serotonin levels. Serotonin is a chemical message transmitter in the brain that improves and stabilises mood. Depressed people often have low serotonin levels, and drugs that increase them can improve depression. Unfortunately, there are potential side effects

to these drugs such as loss of sex drive, headaches, nausea, and most unfortunately and controversially, increased risk of suicide. Exercise has been shown to be as effective as drugs in treating mild depression, and these findings are backed by the Mental Health Foundation.

- Increasing endorphin levels. Endorphins are naturally occurring brain chemicals, and are released when we exercise vigorously. They are similar to morphine in structure, and fill receptor sites in the brain that can also be filled by poppy-derived drugs such as morphine, opium and heroin. Endorphins give a similar euphoric effect but they're free, legal and don't have side effects.

- Increasing concentration, focus and problem-solving abilities. Studies have shown clearly that becoming fit is coupled with improved scores on mental tests, better short-term memory and fewer mistakes at work.

- Decreasing levels of stress hormones. Physical activity enables the body to get rid of adrenaline, noradrenaline and cortisol faster than inactivity. This translates into lower blood pressure, and feelings of calmness and contentedness, which may explain why, when people get fit, they report that many of their relationships improve, too.

You may or may not have known some of the above facts prior to reading this book. Even if you did, you might be among the majority of the population who already know that exercise is great for both physical and mental health – ***but still fail to make exercise a permanent habit***. It is one of the more difficult vitality habits to maintain because even though our bodies work best when we are active, we are also programmed to conserve energy (in the form of stored fat). This programming worked well when we were cave-people who *had* to be active on a daily basis in order to survive – we needed some kind of mechanism to tell us to rest for when our reserves were called on.

Redefine exercise

Now things are different, to say the least. Most of us lead largely sedentary lifestyles, so we have to insert activity *proactively* into our days,
ideally through lots of little bits of informal activity, *and* more formal
exercise sessions. But we are luckier than cave-people, because we can
choose activities that we like. Here's a revelation for you: physical activity
need not be a tedious chore. You can choose something that you find
FUN! In fact, you can stop using the word 'exercise' if you like. Insert
the word 'play', 'fun', 'energiser', 'recreation' or 'release'.

There are ways to 'play' that will suit every personality, body shape,
budget and muscle type. Yes, muscle type. We all have a percentage of
'fast-twitch' and 'slow-twitch' muscle fibres, which is determined geneti-
cally. Someone with more 'fast-twitch' fibres might naturally love racquet
sports, football or any sport requiring short bursts of speed. Someone
with more 'slow-twitch' fibres might love (and find easy) long-distance
running, cycling or swimming.

Don't think you like any sports? Have you really tried them all? Get
down to your local sports centre and try a spinning class, join a volleyball
club or take up yoga. If it suits your budget, try sailing, horse-riding
or windsurfing. If it suits your personality, try the new craze for jive
dancing, start fencing or training in a martial art. The critical thing is
to love it, look forward to it, and maybe even get addicted to it. And
what if you get tired of it? Then – duh – try something new!

The four 'S's of fitness

For complete fitness and maximum vitality, you need to expand your capacity in four fitness arenas I call **The Four 'S's**:

Stamina
Strength
Suppleness
Speed

Stamina

Stamina is all about cardiovascular fitness – the ability of your body to take in and utilise oxygen to burn energy for long periods without fatigue. Both the American Medical Association and British Medical Association emphasise this as the most important form of fitness because it is the type that reduces the risk of heart attacks and strokes.

To increase it, you only need to do rhythmic exercise that uses the major muscle groups (legs, arms and torso) for 30 minutes, three times a week. This is termed 'aerobic' (meaning 'with oxygen') exercise and includes walking briskly, running, cycling, swimming, aerobics classes, dancing continuously, cross-country skiing, skipping, and, well, you get the idea. You should work at a level that makes you breathe hard but not be completely out of breath. A simple way to test this is by trying to speak aloud. If you have to pause to breathe after approximately every seven words, you are working at the right intensity to increase your stamina.

Strength

Strength is the muscles' ability to work against resistance, and is improved through weightlifting, yoga, martial arts, rugby, and activities like heavy gardening work and DIY. It's important to work on it because as we age, we begin to lose muscle size and strength, and this affects functionality and quality of life.

I used to be a competitive triathlete, so I did lots of swimming and weight training. Interesting, though, my upper body is stronger now from doing handstands and other yoga postures, than it ever was from training for triathlons.

There are many different theories about the very best way to improve strength, but a classic weight training programme for strength building would include exercises for all the major muscle groups, and involve doing 2–3 sets of 8–12 repetitions of lifting the weight. The amount of weight chosen for the exercise is based on the ability to do this number of sets and repetitions. There are some excellent books in the resource list at the back of this book to help you build a strength-training programme.

Suppleness

Suppleness is another aspect of fitness that goes away if we don't deliberately maintain it, and greatly affects functionality in later life. I can remember my grandmother having difficulty in lifting things from high shelves because her shoulder flexibility was so limited. You don't have to go very far to see examples of elderly people who have trouble moving fluidly because of lack of flexibility.

Suppleness is enhanced by stretching programmes, yoga, pilates, and through activities such as dancing and gymnastics. But no serious dancer or gymnast (or any serious athlete, for that matter) would be without some sort of suppleness programme in addition to their sport-specific training.

At the risk of sounding like a yoga bore, I cannot recommend it enough for improving suppleness and posture, and reducing tension (particularly in back, neck and shoulders). It makes you feel taller, lighter and more graceful, and as I said above, many of the postures also improve strength. If you try yoga and don't like it, you probably have the wrong teacher for you. Try another yoga class before you give up on it entirely. Although I have added a number of books and DVDs about yoga to the resource list at the back of this book, I strongly recommend that you have a teacher to help you learn the importance nuances of the postures.

Speed

Speed is probably the least important aspect of fitness for generating vitality and wellbeing. But it *is* vital for performance in any sport that involves sprinting or quick reactions such as racquet sports, football, cricket, baseball, volleyball – even table tennis. As explained earlier, these sports are likely to be enjoyed (and dominated) by those people naturally blessed with a high proportion of 'fast-twitch' muscle fibres. They are called 'anaerobic' (without oxygen) sports by exercise physiologists because the muscles work at high levels that require burning glucose (blood sugar) and generating energy without enough oxygen in the muscles. That can't be maintained for very long, of course, and that's why we get out of breath and have to slow down eventually when we sprint. I'm not intending, here, to dampen your enthusiasm for speed sports! Most speed sports also build stamina and strength, and so are great for overall fitness.

To increase speed in any activity, we have to train the muscles to literally 'twitch' more quickly. When we sprint, bound or jump as quickly as we can, we not only build muscle power, we literally create the neuro-muscular (brain–muscle) connections that enable faster twitching. Over time, these connections get stronger, and presto – our muscles will move faster!

Easy exercise

We've been talking about the benefits of formal exercise, but I want to remind you that you *can* build more calorie-burning, heart-pumping and energising movement into your normal daily routine, and as it becomes a habit, it also becomes *easy*. Recent research has given clear indications that short bursts of activity, whether they are 'aerobic' or 'anaerobic' can have a significant positive effect on fitness levels. To get you started thinking about how you can incorporate more activity into your days, here are some ideas:

- Take the stairs! Yes, even if it is a few floors . . .
- Walk up escalators – go on!
- Walk or cycle as many short trips as you can (to the post-box, local store, friends' houses)
- Walk or cycle your commute to work. Once you discover the convenience and reliability of it, you may never go back to sedentary commuting!
- If you do stick to public transport, get off one stop early
- Make a habit of break-time walks
- Walk instead of email
- Play active games with your children. Take them cycling, or ask them to cycle along while you run
- Get a dog that needs walking twice a day, or offer to walk a neighbour's dog
- Do a yoga posture such as tree pose, or tighten your tummy muscles every time you brush your teeth
- When you are walking, lift your torso and breastbone, roll your shoulders back and down, and walk swiftly with purpose
- Dance, stretch and move energetically while you do your chores. Just watch Cameron Diaz in the opening scene of Charlie's Angels!

"I go running when I have to. When the ice cream van is doing 60."
WENDY LIEBMAN

Walking innovations

With our lives becoming increasingly sedentary, there are some movements that are trying to reverse the trend.

A growing number of companies around the world are introducing 'walking meetings' where workers stroll and chat rather than sit around a table. This doesn't work for all types of meetings, but can be particularly effective for creative work and discussion about objectives and goals. Some businesses, schools and hospitals are developing pedometer competitions to see who walks most during a working day.

Many schools have introduced 'walking buses', which are simply groups of children walking to school with adult volunteers. There is a designated route with 'pick-up' points that allow parents to feel safe about their children walking to school. For added safety, the children often wear reflective vests, and younger children can be roped together – so they really do resemble a human bus.

Dr. James Levine, a consultant at the Mayo clinic in Minnesota, USA, has developed a programme whereby school children stand up and move around the classroom for much of the day working at 'lean and move bays' on laptop computers, white boards and vertical screens. This is said to burn up to three times the calories of sitting at traditional desks. Just for the record, the kids do get to sit down on floor cushions to rest sometimes!

Now answer these questions about the activity in your life. You can download a clean copy of the worksheet from **www.stop-making-excuses. com**.

Are you living in a way that will give you the fitness you want to enjoy when you're 70?

✎ ....

....

If you're not, what would you have to do to be able to answer 'yes'?

✎ ....

....

What about right now? How fit do you want to feel in your everyday life now, today?

✎ ....

....

How much time are you willing to give up, in order to have the fitness you want? Circle one of the choices below – but wait, just before you do, here's a reminder – there are 168 hours in each week. You sleep for around 50 of those. How many do you spend working? Watching TV?

Ok, now circle one:

To be honest, none

One hour/week

Two hours/week

Three hours/week

More than that – I have a MEGA fitness goal

The only thing left to ask is: When are you going to start?

And if you answered honestly that you aren't willing to give up any time to be fit, what could you do to change your view? A positive image of a fit you? A negative image of a decrepit you at 70?

✎ ....

....

" *If you can [focus on the nutrition essentials], slowly but surely, your body will start to feel, and look, healthier, stronger and more capable of juggling your demands, and you will feel as if you have a life, rather than being drained by it.* **"**

JANE CLARKE, THE TIMES NUTRITIONIST AND AUTHOR OF
BODYFOODS FOR BUSY PEOPLE

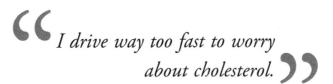

" *I drive way too fast to worry about cholesterol.* **"**

STEVEN WRIGHT, ACADEMY AWARD-WINNING
COMEDIAN, WRITER AND ACTOR

CHAPTER 16

Eat, drink and be energised

One of the greatest pleasures there is in life is the enjoyment of good food and drink. The variety of flavours and textures on this earth is staggering, and it would be a life's work just to experience it all. Yet most of us eat pretty similar stuff week in, week out. We grab junk food on the run and end up with packaged pap when we haven't planned well enough to have fresh food. Why is this? Well, as wonderful as it is, it's not essential we eat interesting, wholesome food. Our bodies can, amazingly, get by on rubbish. Just look around you at the millions of people who do. It isn't great for energy or long-term health, but we can survive. The thing is, though, as far as I'm concerned, survival is **NOT ENOUGH!**

If you want to have high energy levels, stamina, razor sharp focus, creativity and a cheerful mood, the reality is that you've got to fuel yourself accordingly. Think Porsche, not clapped-out banger. But before you start to explain why your life just does not allow for the luxury of decent nutrition, let's bust a couple of common excuses right up front about healthy eating. You do *not* need:

a. *A lot of money* or
b. *A lot of time.*

The cheapest food on earth is local produce in season, and dried staples like beans, legumes, rice and pasta. And the fastest food on earth is not take-aways (if you count travel or delivery time) but things like simple salads and stir-fries.

What you do need in order to eat well is:

a. *a little knowledge (most of which you have already)*
b. *a little organisation* and
c. *some willingness to try new ways of eating.*

A little knowledge

Like I said, you already have a pretty good idea of how to nourish yourself properly. Eat lots of fresh fruits and vegetables, whole grains, beans, pulses, nuts and seeds: limit animal fats, simple sugars, processed food, caffeine and alcohol. Drink plenty of water. Voila. But are you doing this consistently? We'll get to why you might not be in a minute. First let me remind you about why these nutritional principles are what they are.

To maintain energy levels, we need to keep our blood sugar levels within an optimum range: not too low (hypoglycaemia, when we feel low, tired and lack concentration), and not too high (hyperglycaemia, which results in a plunge to hypoglycaemia).

There are big energy benefits for keeping blood sugar levels within the optimum range:

- Better concentration
- Better creativity
- Better and more stable moods
- More stamina
- Less susceptibility to adult-onset diabetes.

To do this, we need to eat little and often (5–8 times per day, no skipping breakfast!), and eat a mixed diet high in complex carbohydrates. Complex carbohydrates are unrefined fruits, vegetables and grains. They take a relatively long time to digest, so energy from them trickles into our systems and blood sugar stays within that optimum range. Simple, or refined carbohydrates (biscuits, sweets, chocolate, sugary drinks, alcohol) rush into the bloodstream and result in hyperglycaemia, as described above. Too many of my clients end up on a blood sugar roller coaster when they eat high-sugar snacks and eat too infrequently.

Along with carbohydrate we need to be eating protein and healthy fats, too, because they slow the absorption of carbohydrates, help to maintain weight (yes, really) and improve brain function. When you look down at your plate of food, you should ideally be eating 60% carbohydrate, most of this coming from fruits and vegetables, and 40% protein-rich foods. Both the carbs and the protein foods you choose should bring with them healthy fats – we're talking avocados, nuts, seeds, oily fish and lean meats.

After 18 years of working with people who need peak mental performance five to seven days a week, I believe that this diet is ideal, and the best resource I know of to learn about it is *The Food Doctor Everyday Diet* by Ian Marber. It explains the benefits of this diet clearly, shows you the pitfalls of other diets, and has some simple, yummy recipes to boot.

> **Complex carbohydrate has 3.75 kilocalories per gram, protein has 4, and fat has 9!**
>
> That doesn't mean you should avoid fat entirely, just be aware that you don't have to eat much before you have stacked up the calories. Nuts and seeds, for instance, are healthy, high-energy snacks, but tend to be high in fat, so we don't need to eat many to get a decent dose of calories.

And just one more thing: find a way to incorporate peas, beans, lentils and soybeans into your diet. They are excellent sources of protein, carbohydrate, fibre and a range of phytonutrients: awesome compounds with amazing properties that protect against all manner of illnesses, particularly cancer. Don't imagine bowls of plain lentils. Put chickpeas into your curries and kidney beans into chilli. Eat bean and vegetable soups, and good ol' beans on toast.

PS. Fruits and vegetables are bursting with phytonutrients, too.

A little organisation

You **do** have time to eat healthily. It is no good saying that you don't have time to eat breakfast, or a healthy snack at mid-morning, but you do have time for another double espresso and a chocolate biscuit. Breakfast can be a piece of fruit and a store-bought smoothie, and if your stomach doesn't want food first thing in the morning, then eat as early as you're able. See the 'Power Foods' pin-up at the end of this chapter and at **www.stop-making-excuses.com** for easy meal ideas.

Even if you don't pack your entire lunch before work, you can still take some fruit, oatcakes, dried fruit and nuts, and herbal tea bags to work with very little time input. For just a few more minutes, you could make your own healthy lunch. If your staff canteen doesn't serve you what you want, ask nicely for it. And don't give up after the initial response of 'sorry, we don't do that'.

Buy your non-perishable snacks in bulk, and stash them in a desk drawer. If you have something you like to hand, you'll be less likely to resort to chocolate or crisps.

If you find that dinner is the meal that blows your good nutritional intentions, then line up your week's evening meals over the weekend, and shop accordingly. You can cook big batches of things like vegetable curries and pasta sauces, then freeze in portions. If this seems way too structured for you then get yourself a super-fast healthy recipe book (there are a few I suggest in the resource list at the end of the book). Again, make sure you have the ingredients you'll need for the week. If you 'can't cook, won't cook', then get good at reading labels on ready-meals. There are healthy pasta and stir-fry sauces, ready-meals and soups on the market, but you have to look carefully at the content. Obviously steer clear of cream sauces and fried foods.

Look for (per portion):

- Salt content less than 1 g
- Saturated fat content less than 6–10 g

The total recommended daily intake of fat is 95 g for men, and 70 g for women – and only 30 g and 20 g (or less), respectively, should be saturated fat.

- Simple sugars less than 15 g

The label will say something like: carbohydrate 15.8 g, of which sugars 2.5 g. It's the 'sugars' that should be the low number.

My nutritional therapist friend Natalie Gotts says that you should forget about numbers entirely, and just make sure that what you choose is high in protein and fibre: lean meats, fish, pulses and beans, and vegetables. Make sure the label has ingredients that are real food and not chemicals you think belong in a chemistry lab.

Eat differently

I'm always fascinated when people say to me, 'Well, I just don't like . . . vegetables, fruit, beans, nuts, whole wheat bread, brown rice . . . whatever'. I guess that just leaves doughnuts, then. People tell me they can't cook, so obviously they have to eat take-away curry every night. And they simply can't control their cravings for chocolate, so it isn't their fault that's all they snack on. When you see it in black and white, it's obvious how stupid these excuses are.

Ultimately, how you fuel your body has a huge impact on every aspect of your energy levels. So, if you don't have all the energy you want, and your diet isn't that great, you clearly need to make some changes. And that might mean learning to like foods that you currently don't, or learning to cook, or learning to enjoy cooking!

Only 5-a-day?

My daughter's piano teacher, Sue, battled breast cancer several years ago, and it changed her way of living and eating dramatically. Before the diagnosis, she typically ate (and fed her family) high-fat meals from the freezer, with no emphasis on fresh fruits and vegetables, and no worries about additives or transfats. When she became ill, she started educating herself about healthy eating. Now she doesn't just get her 5-a-day, she shoots for 7–10 portions of fresh fruits and vegetables every single day. This was such a radical departure from her previous way of life that she kept a wall chart for the first seven months to count her daily portions. Now it has become a natural way of life, along with at least two portions of oily fish a week, more pulses, lots of water, and the elimination of dairy products.

Here's what Sue says about the transformation of her palate: 'Before cancer I would say "I know I should eat better, but I do like this and that". And "I can't live without that". I would have said "fish is bland" or "I can only eat fish in batter", but you have to rethink your diet and find your own fast food. To make a shift you don't say, "I can't eat chocolate or Indian takeaway." You are saying, "Whatever else you do, do this **first**." People think they like fast food, but they can like good stuff. Your taste buds can change!'

I'll let you in on a couple of secrets, though. It's not so hard learning to like wholesome food. Your body, deep down, loves what's good for it. BUT, it will also crave sugar, salt and bad fats if that's what you normally feed it. Weird, but true.

And cooking isn't difficult, either. It's just cutting food up and mixing it together in a pan with some herbs and spices. If it freaks you out, get a fail-safe, basic cookery book. If you 'hate' cooking, then find a way to make it enjoyable. Listen to your favourite music, or an audio-book to distract you from your task.

Here are some more suggestions for contemplating fuelling yourself in a more energising way:

- Think about when during the day you consume most of your calories, and why. Are you a 'back-end loader', consuming most of your daily calories after 8 pm? Could you try eating more during the working day and less in the evening? You can still have your social meal with partner or friends – you just won't need to eat as much.
- Do you give in to temptations around 4 pm when you need not only calories but a morale boost as well? How could you plan your eating better?
- If you never eat breakfast, could you try it and see how you feel? Perhaps just something very small to start with, building up to a more substantial energy intake if you find it does you good.

- Could you reduce your intake of chocolate, crisps, alcohol, caffeine, or whatever it is that is throwing you out of balance? Yes, enjoy those things occasionally – just don't try to live on them.

Weight loss

So many volumes have been written on this subject that I couldn't hope to refute or verify every theory out there. Here's what I think:

If you're overweight, and you're unhappy about it, it's probably depleting your emotional and spiritual energies more than your physical energy. If you're carrying some extra pounds but truly happy with your body, then it may not be a problem at all. You don't have to be super thin to be healthy and have stacks of energy.

If you're clinically 'overweight' or 'obese' (definitions at the end of this chapter), don't kid yourself that it's just a few extra pounds. This kind of overweight greatly increases your chances of having pain in various bits of your body, and very 'uncool' and dangerous conditions like adult-onset diabetes, arthritis, chronic fatigue syndrome, angina, heart disease and other vascular disease. These illnesses take a tremendous amount of energy just to cope with and control, so there's not a lot left over for the things you really want to do.

So what do you do?

It's a basic physical law that energy can neither be created nor destroyed. So to lose weight, you have to consume a little less than you expend. You might need to feel a little bit hungry for a while. I'm **not** talking starvation, of course. My recommendations for losing weight are:

- Stop eating **before** you feel totally full
- Eat 'mindfully' – that is, fully chew and taste each mouthful, and put down your utensils between every bite
- Eat 5–8 small meals a day
- Eat **even more** vegetables – they fill up your stomach with fibre and water, and give you oodles of nutrition to boot
- Give up the junk for a while – yes, all of it
- Learn the difference between hunger and boredom, hunger and needing comfort, hunger and just the pleasure of eating
- In the long term, re-educate your body's appestat so that you naturally eat as much as you expend. Guess how you do that? Through exercise and healthy eating. No surprises there.

Increasing activity really is the way to shift the pounds because it increases both your overall metabolism and the amount of fat you're burning. It's not instant weight loss, but it's much more likely to be permanent.

It's worth noting that gym equipment notoriously gives quite inflated figures for calorie burning. Working on an elliptical trainer does *not* burn 700 calories per hour! More like 360, and that's if you are working pretty hard. So, if you do an hour every day for 10 days, and don't change your diet at all, you'll have theoretically lost one and a bit pounds. But don't we all like to see faster results than that? Hardly worth it, you might squawk. Well, that's just the way it is. One pound is equal to about 3500 calories. You can go on a much more calorie-restricted diet to lose weight faster, but that should be under the supervision of a doctor or an accredited weight loss counsellor.

A monumental step to a size 10

A friend of mine, Jenny, lost an incredible amount of weight – almost 6 stone in 4½ months. That's the sort of rapid loss that should be properly supervised, and Jenny was. She used a programme that replaced all meals with nutritionally complete supplements, shakes and soups. She told me that this system 'suited the way her brain works'. For her, it was easier to completely focus on what this diet provided and not have to worry about portions of 'normal' food. This eliminated temptation to keep eating, or sneak a little of the bad stuff. The way she speaks about the experience, it's clear that she made a firm decision to go on this diet with no cheating. She said that if you 'cheat' on a diet, all you're doing is deceiving yourself. You might make an adult decision to enjoy some ice cream or chocolate, but that is different to being childlike and defying the authority of the diet.

The benefits of her weight loss are amazing, as you can imagine. 'Now my husband pursues me around the house', she said. Plus she does more for herself like massages and float tank sessions – when we spoke she had bookings for both the following week. She goes to the gym regularly, and loves the energy of being fitter. She told me that she didn't notice the lack of fitness when she was overweight. 'When it happens gradually, you gradually adapt to both the weight and to being unfit. But now, I can really feel the difference!'

Psychologically, being able to stick rigorously to the diet plan – even over Christmas and New Year – has given Jenny a new confidence, not to mention all the praise that continues when friends see her.

My observation is that she is a new woman on the inside, too, more relaxed and *much* happier!

Another way to look at weight gain is that if you eat just one digestive biscuit (74 calories) over and above your daily calorie requirement, you'd put on half a stone each year. So when overweight people say 'I really don't eat that much', they are often telling the truth . . . but, they're still eating more than they're expending.

The bottom line here is that we all need to reassess portion sizes and start 'downsizing'. 'Large' portion sizes these days are often enough for three people. Restaurants sometimes dish up mountains of food, while we stay stuck in the 'think of the starving children in Africa' mentality.

Some weight loss programmes, including the one that Jenny used include cognitive behavioural therapy techniques and transactional analysis to help people think differently about food. For instance, if you feel obliged to eat everything on your plate, or eat up leftovers, you need to reprogramme your brain with new messages about how it is worse to be a human garbage disposal than it is to waste food. Do you use excuses like, 'I deserve ice cream because I've had a hard day', or 'it's okay to eat this because it's a special party.' Again, you need new thoughts about how great it feels to feed your body healthily and not stuff it full of sugar or fat. If you're stuck in child-like naughtiness or rebellion, consider how much this looks like cutting off your nose to spite your face. Whatever you do, lose weight *for you*, not for anyone else. And do it to *feel awesome*.

> *If you get to a point where you see food simply as something that will make you fat or thin, then your vision has become blurred.*
> IAN MARBER, *THE FOOD DOCTOR EVERYDAY DIET*

Body Mass Index

To calculate whether you are overweight, divide your weight in kilograms by your height in metres squared (body weight / height^2). This is known as your Body Mass Index or BMI. This doesn't work if you are extremely muscular, but if that's you, you know who you are. The classifications are:

- 30 Clinical obesity
- >28 Clinical obesity when other certain medical conditions are present
- 25–29.9 Overweight. There is a significant increase in the risk of obesity-related diseases
- 18.5–24.9 Most appropriate for long-term health

LIVE WITH ENERGY PIN-UP

Power Foods – Enjoy your food, enjoy the energy

This is a list of suggested foods for maximising your energy. You can print a copy from **www.stop-making-excuses.com**. For lots more creative and fun recipe suggestions, go to the website, or see the list of suggested cookbooks in the resource list at the back of this book.

Breakfasts

- **Wholemeal cereals** with no added sugar. Add your own nuts, and fruit to sweeten. Moisten with milk or be adventurous and try rice milk, soy milk or fruit juice.
- **Wholemeal toast** with:
  - no-sugar jam (try St. Dalfour – gorgeous stuff) or honey
  - nut butter – choose an unsweetened variety made from nuts other than peanuts
  - butter or margarine with no hydrogenated fats – sparingly.
- **Eggs**
- **Fruit salad** with yoghurt (live-culture yoghurt may help to prevent colds and be good for digestion).
- **Smoothies** – home-made, or a commercial variety with no added sugar or fruit juice concentrates.

- **Porridge!** This is one of the most sustaining breakfasts you can eat. Forget any bad experiences of this energising food. Cook some up with chopped banana, orange, raisins, cinnamon and nutmeg; sweeten with a little honey and you have a real power breakfast. To save time in the morning, prepare and soak overnight.

Lunches

- **Wholemeal bread sandwiches** with salmon, sardines, tuna, chicken, lean beef, cheese, chutney, roasted vegetables, hummus, lettuce, rocket, tomato, grated carrot . . .
- **Salads** with the addition of nuts, legumes (black, kidney, cannellini and haricot beans, peas, chickpeas, lentils and soybeans), grains like bulgar wheat (found in many Mediterranean dishes), or avocado (high in monounsaturated fat – a healthy one).
- **Baked potatoes** with beans, cottage cheese, yoghurt, chives and/or any veggies.
- **Healthy soups** – low fat and low salt, high in vegetables, beans and grains such as barley. Look for products that have less than 10 g of fat and less than 400 mg sodium per serving.
- **Cheese and oatcakes**, with chutney and fruit or salad. Just remember cheese is high in calories, but this is a very sustaining lunch.
- **Crudités and hummus or guacamole dip**
- **Falafel** as a spread or baked as little balls. They're made from chickpeas and delicious with salsa or a yoghurt dip.
- **Peppered smoked mackerel** or any oily fish with any of the above to accompany it.

Snacks

- **Crudités** with yoghurt or other low-fat dip.
- **Fruit** is a perfect snack – high in fructose (fruit sugar that does not give the same sugar 'high'), water-soluble vitamins (B's and C),

potassium, fibre and numerous 'phytochemicals' (compounds known to help prevent cancer and other serious diseases).

- **Dried fruit** has the same benefits with a small loss of Vitamin C. It is sweeter, and also higher in calories since the water is gone. Enjoy, just watch the quantities!
- **Tinned fruit**, packed in natural juice. Look for small, snack-sized tins.
- **Nuts** – particularly:
    - Brazil – high in magnesium, important in energy release and nutrient absorption, and selenium, an antioxidant also key in keeping skin and hair healthy
    - Cashew – high in zinc (for a strong immune system and wound healing), and magnesium
    - Macadamia – high in magnesium
    - Walnuts – high in B-vitamins, magnesium and antioxidant vitamin E (which also boosts immune system)
    - Pine nuts – high in zinc
    - Hazelnuts – high in vitamin E
    - Almonds – high in vitamin E, magnesium, iron, calcium and potassium.
- **Seeds** – particularly:
    - Pumpkin – high in zinc
    - Sunflower – high in magnesium, iron, B-vitamins and vitamin E
    - Sesame – high in magnesium.
- **Approved seed mixes include:**
    - Lawncourt Harvest Munchy Seeds
    - Clearspring Roasted Seed and Soya Snacks
    - You Are What You Eat' Sensational Natural Seed Mix & Fruit and Nut Snack Mix
    - Food doctor Original 5-Seed Mix.
- **Energy bars** with no added sugar (in its many guises) or hydrogenated vegetable fat. Approved brands include:
    - Wallaby

- Fruitas (made by Lyme Regis foods)
- Fruitina
- Orgran
- Lara
- 'O'
- Nakd
- Bounce Balls (look gross but taste delicious if you like marzipan)
- Taste of Nature.

- **Yoghurt and fromage frais** – low-fat if you are watching calories, and no added sugar.
- **Bagels** – find wholemeal/seed varieties.
- Occasionally, **chocolate**. It does contain antioxidants, believe it or not, and its fat, stearic acid, is not bad for your arteries. Go for dark chocolate, as it has more flavonoids (phytonutrients that actually reduce the risk of heart disease).

Dinners

- You should not arrive at this meal famished! Eat more throughout the day and eat less here. And remember, large quantities of red meat, fat, salt and/or alcohol will sap tomorrow's energy.
- **Pasta** (ideally whole meal – try it!) and **low-fat sauce that has a source of protein** such as beans, fish or lean meat. Don't forget the salad on the side.
- **Fish!** We should all eat more oily fish such as tuna, salmon, mackerel, sardines.
- **Stir-fries**. The possibilities are endless for ingredients, and there are some yummy and healthy stir-fry sauces on the market. Add ginger for its natural anti-inflammatory properties. Add garlic for cholesterol reduction, blood thinning and cancer protection. Use sesame, canola, olive or flaxseed oil for stir-fries.
- **Rice-based dishes like chilli and curry**. Try some vegetarian options, and use brown rice. Easy-cook brown rice only takes 20 minutes to cook, and is far better for energy than the white variety.

- **Vegetarian omelettes**
- **Salads** with cheese, nuts or beans.
- Add lots of colourful vegetables to your plate. Think red, orange, yellow, green, dark green, purple. Every colour has its own brand of mega healthy phytonutrient, and every type of phytonutrient reduces the risk of some kind of yucky disease.

Puddings

- **Fruit salad** – treat yourself to some exotic fruit and this will make it seem special.
- A few squares of **dark chocolate**.
- **Baked apples** stuffed with dried fruit.
- Very small portions of naughty puddings (yes, a little of what you fancy does you good).

Drinks

- **Water**, of course.
- **Herbal teas**. Ginger, ginseng, lemon, orange, cardamom, cloves, liquorice and cinnamon are all particularly energy-boosting. Chamomile, lavender, rose and valerian are calming; peppermint aids digestion and helps an upset stomach. Try Yogi, Pukka, Clipper and Qi brands.
- **Green tea**, high in antioxidants, and very low caffeine.

"*Even small amounts of sleep debt . . . have a significant impact on strength, cardiovascular capacity, mood and overall energy levels. Some fifty studies have shown that mental performance – reaction time, concentration, memory and logical/ analytical reasoning – all decline steadily as sleep debt increases.*"

JIM LOEHR AND TONY SCHWARTZ, IN *ON FORM*

"*If your husband has difficulty in getting to sleep, the words, 'We need to talk about our relationship' may help.*"

RITA RUDNER, COMEDIAN

CHAPTER 17

Sleeping beauty

ran into a girlfriend the other day, and naturally asked how she was doing. 'I'm so tired', she replied. 'I'm just not sleeping at the moment. I've got a big project on at work and I wake up every morning at 4:30 stressing about it!' Does this sound familiar?

It's got to be one of the most miserable feelings in the world to have to struggle through another day of commitments, deadlines, parenting or other caring responsibilities on a poor night's sleep. Whether it's waking at 4:30 am, sleeping fitfully or not being able to get to sleep at all, if you're sleep-deprived, you quickly realise that sleep is the single most critical aspect of your health and energy management, ultimately more important than diet or exercise. Sleep deprivation wrecks your vitality, your moods, your concentration and creativity. It damages the immune system, reduces cell repair and fertility, and makes you more stressed.

Studies show that over a third of us do not get sufficient sleep, and millions are spent on sleeping tablets and remedies, which is testament to the fact that too many people just aren't getting a full forty winks.

But how much is enough? People vary enormously in the amount they need, from Maggie Thatcher's four hours to your teenager's ten. Sleep experts agree that it's not about a certain number of hours. The real question to ask yourself is: 'Do I feel refreshed and rested after being awake for 30 minutes or so?' If the answer is 'Yes', then no problem. If not, it could be lack of *quantity . . . or quality*.

You might think that lack of *quantity* is simply a case of scheduling. Just go to bed earlier, right? But it isn't always that simple. If you get home from work after 8 pm, it's unlikely you'll be ready to drop off until 11, because of the time it takes to cook, eat, have a bit of an 'evening' that you feel entitled to, then wind down enough to slip off to la-la land. People get into patterns where they aren't 'ready' to sleep until a late hour, even if, deep down, they are truly tired. I call this 'tired but wired' and it's no joke.

The more these patterns are reinforced, the harder it is to go to sleep earlier because it establishes a 'circadian' rhythm. Circadian means 'about a day' and is the rhythm of when we wake, sleep and feel hungry. It is influenced mostly by light, but also by noise, pressure to perform, food and individual biochemistry. One important hormone controlled by circadian rhythms is melatonin (used by many jet-setters to help recover from jet lag). The more melatonin you produce, the sleepier you feel and the deeper your slumber can be. If you don't normally go to bed until 11 or later, you probably won't be producing enough melatonin to go to sleep any earlier, at least not until you can 'shift' your day back to the left, rather like changing time zones.

Not only that, but any pressure on you, self-imposed or otherwise, reduces melatonin production and increases production of stress hormones (adrenaline, noradrenaline and cortisol). They increase your alertness and readiness for action, which obviously affects whether you can sleep at all, as well as the *depth* of sleep you can reach. As I'm sure you've experienced, no matter how many hours you sleep, what really counts is the **quality** of your sleep.

I'm not making this up

Recent research has shown that lack of sleep can make you fat! With sleep deprivation, we release less leptin, a hormone that signals the state of fat stores, and more ghrelin, a hormone that signals hunger. So without enough shut-eye, we're likely to start overeating. It's just not fair, is it?

To get good quality sleep, start by checking the basics, because unless you get them right, no amount of counting sheep will help you. The first question I ask sleep-deprived clients is, 'How much caffeine do you drink?' Caffeine has the same effect on your nervous system as stress hormones, so if you're a real coffee, tea or coke drinker, I strongly recommend you try **zero** caffeine for at least two weeks to test whether this improves your sleep patterns. If you are major league caffeine user, and want to avoid withdrawal headaches, try cutting caffeine by half, then going to zero a week later.

Jason came to me with low energy levels, initially concerned that his eating habits were not keeping him going through his long work days. Almost as an afterthought he told me he had been insomniac for many years. Well, hello, maybe *that's* why you don't have enough energy, Jason. So, first question: 'How much caffeine do you drink?' He said he only had one, sometimes two cups of tea a day, and never after 1 pm, so that couldn't be causing the insomnia. I talked him into giving up caffeine altogether. Then for various reasons I didn't see him for three weeks. When I did, he was so excited to tell me that it was now taking him less than five minutes to be sound asleep, whereas before it could take up to three hours. He told me he couldn't believe that so little caffeine had impaired his ability to sleep so profoundly. He also said, 'I don't want to sound like a girl, but I have to say, my skin is looking fantastic, and the dark circles under my eyes are gone.' That's the power of a good night's sleep.

The second thing I ask clients is about alcohol consumption because (sorry to tell you this) it also greatly decreases the quality of your sleep. I know, I know, it seems that after a few drinks you sleep like a baby, but in fact it disrupts normal sleep patterns and limits deep restorative sleep. I'm not saying here that you must become teetotal, just be aware of the effect alcohol has, and make your choice. Do you want that third glass of wine or some quality sleep?

The other basic things you must get right for a great night's sleep are:

- Don't eat within an hour of going to bed, because you can't sleep deeply if you're digesting food. *'Eat lite at nite'* is the motto, so don't arrive home starving. Eat more during your working day when your metabolic rate is higher – you need the calories anyway at this time to maintain concentration and a happy, positive mood
- Don't exercise within an hour of going to bed, because you can't sleep deeply if your core temperature is too high

- Don't do household accounts or other administration with 30–60 minutes of trying to sleep.

Nite, nite. Sleep tight.

The origin of the expression 'sleep tight' comes from a time when straw mattresses were suspended inside the bed frame on ropes that criss-crossed underneath. Over time (and due to the weight of the sleepers) the ropes would slacken, and have to be *retightened*, so that the mattress remained comfortable – well, about as comfortable as a straw mattress can get! Next time you're lying awake, focus on the amazing comfort of your modern, sprung mattress.

If you've already sorted out all the basics, and you're still not 'sleeping tight', the following is a range of ideas that might help to improve both the **quantity and quality** of your sleep. Try what your intuition tells you might help.

- Take regular breaks during the day, because they help your brain to sift through and process incoming information, a bit like what you do when you dream. If you take no breaks, you'll need more Rapid Eye Movement (dreaming) sleep at night, and this leaves less time for deep, restorative sleep.
- Have a wind down routine in the evening. Create some rituals that signal to your body that you are going to sleep soon, to embed the right 'circadian rhythm'. This might include light reading, calming yoga postures or a warm bath (not too hot, or your core temperature will get too high, as above).
- Listen to relaxing music (not Metallica, like one client of mine). Definitely use the music that **you** find relaxing, but I can tell you that music of around 60 beats per minute (such as Baroque classical) has been found to slow both heart rate and brain wave frequency.

- Use low-lighting from two hours before bedtime. Avoid overhead lights and install dimmer switches for your lamps. Brush your teeth by candle-light!
- Try drinking chamomile, valerian or St. John's Wort teas, all of which are mild sedatives.
- Ensure you have good ventilation in your bedroom. Better to have a thicker duvet or more blankets than a less than optimum amount of oxygen.
- Tidy your bedroom. Clutter will keep your brain from fully relaxing. And absolutely **no work** in the bedroom. Keep your briefcase out, and no laptops in bed. This might have a positive effect on your relationship, too!
- Try aromatherapy. Have fun using lavender, ylang-ylang, clary sage, neroli or a blended oil designed for relaxation. You don't need an oil burner. Just put a few drops in a mug of hot water or your bath.
- Use a relaxation technique to get to sleep, and to get back to sleep if you wake in the night. Try tracks 5–7 on the Live with Energy CD.

And finally, if you wake in the night:

- Don't whatever you do, turn on the light unless not to do so would be hazardous (e.g. to get to the loo). You'll start up your awake cycle.
- Don't look at the clock! You'll start calculating the hours left till the alarm goes off, and just become more alert. Turn the clock face away from you.
- Choose a specific thing you focus on, such as waves lapping on a shore, a waterfall, soft clouds or even a velvet-covered waterbed – whatever keeps you in a sleep-like state.
- Don't lie awake being angry about it – change your perception. Think 'I am resting peacefully.' Insomniacs sleep for more hours than they perceive they do, and the aim is to relax and rest the brain as much as possible. Worry and anger really *will* make you feel tired tomorrow!

That's an awful lot of information about sleep, I know. The thing is, if you aren't sleeping well, what are you going to do about it? Answer the questions here or download a clean copy from **www.stop-making-excuses. com**.

What rituals will you put in place to ensure a restorative nights' sleep?

....

....

Is there anything you need to stop doing in order to wind down more effectively?

....

....

How will you make these new habits stick?

....

....

It is not a chore, an obligation, or a regime you have to adhere to. It is simply a pleasure. Sheer, unadulterated, guilt-free pleasure. Indeed, to be absolutely relaxed and peaceful is one of the most rewarding, most uplifting experiences a human being can have.

PAUL WILSON, *CALM FOR LIFE*

Try to relax and enjoy the crisis.

BRILLIANT ASHLEIGH, AUTHOR AND CARTOONIST

CHAPTER 18

Relax to renew

Kerri came to one of my stress management workshops in a pretty tense state. Arms folded defensively, I knew I had my work cut out for me to get her to buy into any of the ideas I had to offer. As the workshop progressed, though, she loosened up and shared that she'd just come back to work after three months off with stress-induced depression. She wanted to learn how to prevent this happening again, but she said that she absolutely 'could not relax'. I asked her what she'd tried, and she proudly told me that she had taken a course in meditation. My next question was, 'how long have you been practising it?' and it turned out she had only stuck at it for a week after the course. Because she found her mind drifted, she decided relaxation was impossible. I told her that Zen masters find their minds drift too, and then she got a different perspective.

One thing I've noticed in 18 years of health consultancy is that those people who have a specific, regular way to relax are far more resilient to stress and have more energy than those who don't. It doesn't take a PhD to figure out the connection . . . so why is it that so few of us take time out to really relax each day?

And when I say relax, I mean true, deep relaxation. Watching 'Eastenders' doesn't count! TV might be great recreation, but it doesn't give your brain or your body the amazing benefits of deep relaxation.

Let me explain. For humans, deep relaxation occurs only with certain frequencies of brain activity. The brain emits four types of waves, each with its own characteristic rhythm or frequency range:

BETA waves (14–40 cycles per second) are the ordinary conscious rhythms. They predominate when attention is directed to the outside world, and we are alert and focussed.

ALPHA waves (8–13 cycles per second) are present during dreaming and light meditation. They reflect calmness and introspection, and enhance creativity.

THETA waves (4–7 cycles per second) are associated with deep physical relaxation and emotional tranquillity.

DELTA waves (.5–3 cycles per second) are present in deep sleep when our bodies are repairing and recovering.

Deep relaxation, unlike sleep, produces a predominance of alpha and theta rhythms indicating a state of harmony and bliss – but you don't just get them happening by accident. You have to proactively decide to relax, and do something to promote it.

But why bother?

Lots of people tell me that they're 'happy being busy', 'don't like to sit down', or that they're not stressed, so they don't need to relax. I used to be like that, too, so I understand completely. Secretly, I was worried that I might get bored and that I'd be 'wasting' precious achievement time. Hmmm.

Well, here are some benefits to relaxation that might make you consider investing just 10–20 minutes a day:

- Serotonin levels increase – serotonin is a neurotransmitter that is associated with calmness and happiness. Low serotonin levels are linked with depression
- Blood pressure decreases
- Stress hormone levels decrease
- Your immune system strengthens. Research has shown an increase in the activity of 'natural killer cells' that kill bacteria and cancer cells during and after meditation
- Brain waves in the stress-prone right frontal brain cortex move to the calmer left frontal cortex
- Analytical ability increases
- Creativity increases.

Over the long term:

- Risk of stress-related illness decreases
- Sleep quality increases and amount of sleep needed decreases.

In fact, relaxation for five to ten minutes can be more effective than sleep in leaving you feeling refreshed and energised. We'll be talking about breaks in the next chapter.

If you're willing to try relaxation, it's incredibly simple. No lotus position or incense required. If you're willing to stick at for longer than just a

week like Kerri, I promise you that you'll be amazed at the results. The list above has all the benefits that can be tested scientifically. What it doesn't say is that people who do some form of deep relaxation regularly report higher levels of inner peace, happiness, love, guidance and wisdom.

OK, how do I get started then?

To relax deeply, all you have to do is sit quietly and comfortably, and focus on your breathing. Get comfortable, deliberately begin to let go of tension, and try to breathe from your belly rather than your chest. In other words, let the air flow to the bottom and outer reaches of your lungs rather than just the top half. Simply feel the air enter your nose, windpipe and lungs, and feel it leave. Notice the coolness of the air as it enters; notice the warmth as it leaves. When your mind wanders, don't worry about it. Just come back to your breath. It's as simple as that, but as Kerri's story illustrated, it takes practice and getting used to. There's no right or wrong – only how you feel during and after the process.

But shouldn't I take a course?

It can be very helpful to take a meditation course such as Transcendental Meditation, or buy a CD to help you, but it's not necessary. There are lots of ways to meditate, and there's plenty of information on the web for you to explore.

The following are some of the more popular ways to relax or meditate that you can try:

Focussed meditation

Just as the method above focussed on the breath, you can focus on many different things:

- A word, or *mantra* such as 'calm', 'love', 'peace' or 'om'.
- A beautiful object – but without trying to describe it in your head
- A mundane object – in order to clear your head
- A candle, or just the image of a candle in your head
- The sound of a metronome
- The sound of ocean waves (probably from a CD unless you have beach-front property!)
- Counting slowly to 10 over and over.

Mindfulness meditation

This is about staying in the present moment, and being aware of what you are feeling physically and emotionally in every moment moving forward. This frees you of the need to spend energy on rehashing the past or worrying about the future.

Spiritual meditation

People with a spiritual belief can use meditation as a form of prayer. A prayer can be repeated over and over as a form of mantra, or the meditator can speak to God and then wait peacefully for guidance.

Creative visualisation

In this form of meditation, you simply imagine peaceful, happy surroundings such as the beach, a lake or a mountain top, and you experience all the sights, sounds, smells and physical aspects of that place *internally*. Tracks 5–7 on the Live with Energy CD are creative visualisations for relaxation. They couldn't be simpler. All you have to do is listen and follow my voice. If you find it difficult to get into it at first, remember that if you rarely relax, then your body and brain may be resistant to it. Give yourself a few sessions to get used to it.

Plenty of my clients think that 'this meditation stuff' is not for them, but many top athletes, such as Serena Williams, business people such as the late Sir John Harvey Jones and stars Shania Twain and Richard Gere use this powerful way to renew, and sharpen up both physically and mentally.

It can do the same for you, and keep you from ending up where Kerri did. But the story ended happily for her. She now has my guided imagery CD that she uses every day after work, and swears by.

Over to you, now. You can answer these questions here or download a clean copy from **www.stop-making-excuses.com**.

Think about how relaxation might make a difference to where you sit on that 1–10 energy scale . . .

What form of relaxation would you be willing to try?

✍ ....

....

OK, when will you try it?

✍ ....

....

How will you maintain it for at least three weeks to see if it makes a difference to your energy and your life?

✍ ....

....

How will you banish guilt about 'doing nothing'?

✍ ....

....

Now go and schedule it into your diary.

Seriously. Do it right now, or the moment will pass and you won't do it. Relaxing isn't imperative, so it's not going to happen unless you do it proactively. Where will it really fit into your busy schedule? First thing in the morning? Last thing before bed? Over lunch, when you arrive home?

"When people moan, 'Oh, I'm so busy, I'm run off my feet, my life is a blur, I haven't got time for anything', what they often mean is, 'Look at me: I am hugely important, exciting and energetic.'"

CARL HONORE, *IN PRAISE OF SLOW*

"Do Lipton employees take coffee breaks?"

STEPHEN WRIGHT, COMEDIAN

CHAPTER 19

Have a break

D o you ever find yourself staring at your computer screen, kind of blankly, not focussing on anything in particular? You're not being lazy (probably!) – you've just come to a 'low' or 'rest' phase of your natural energy cycle. These cycles repeat every 90 minutes or so, and they're called *ultradian rhythms*. Ignore them at your peril, because they serve some important functions for your energy levels, concentration, physical and mental health.

In **Chapter 17 – Sleeping beauty**, I mentioned *circadian rhythms*, the daily energy cycles that determine sleepiness, mood, metabolic rate and hunger. They are ultimately set by the sun, of course, and that's why these parameters get confused when you change time zones. Circadian means 'about a day' whereas ultradian simply means 'more than once a day'.

Also called the **basic rest-activity cycle (BRAC)**, these ultradian rhythms occur about 16 times a day – four or five of them while you're sleeping. They were originally discovered by sleep scientists who noted a pattern of 90 minutes of deep dreamless sleep followed by a short period of dreaming. They wondered if we had similar daytime patterns, and surprise, surprise – we do!

So what has this got to do with your energy and wellbeing?

Well, ultradian rhythms are the body's way of getting rest and renewal in between bursts of alertness and activity. To maintain maximum vitality and mental effectiveness, we should honour the body's wisdom and work in sync with them, not try to override them.

But, being human, we tend to ignore the need for breaks. We grab another coffee or sugary snack, or berate ourselves for not keeping up the pace. When we ignore our natural ultradian energy cycles, it's detrimental to our energy in **four important ways:**

Mental Energy

First, our brains lose concentration after about 90 continuous minutes of work, less if it's intense concentration. Air traffic controllers aren't allowed shifts of more than two hours without a break (don't do the maths here – too scary), and minefield clearance operators work in even shorter 20-minute shifts! I'm guessing your work isn't life or death stuff, but if you aren't taking breaks about every 90 minutes, your mental energy will reduce to the point that it takes twice as long to complete a task. From a time management perspective, you're better off having the break and enjoying it.

Rejuvenation

Secondly, breaks are short opportunities for what's called your **parasympathetic nervous system** to come into play, taking care of many critical background maintenance functions such as cell repair, digestion, mood balancing, immune system function – even fertility and libido. This parasympathetic nervous system is pretty much switched off when we're in 'go' mode. During these active phases, it's the complementary **sympathetic nervous system** that is directing the orchestra of your body, keeping your mind sharp, senses alert, muscles tense and ready for action.

When you're stressed, the sympathetic nervous system is even more geared up, cutting out the parasympathetic too much of the time, often resulting in illness. Understanding the yin and yang of the parasympathetic and sympathetic makes it easy to see why 'no breaks' equals stomach aches, headaches, susceptibility to viruses and depression, to name just a few typical stress-related illnesses.

Sleep Quality

Third, 'no breaks' also means poor sleep. As I talked about in Chapter 17, each mental break you take gives your brain the opportunity to consolidate information that you've assimilated or created. It's as if you're organising your documents into files on your hard drive, and discarding information you don't need. This not only gives you a cleaner slate when you return to work, it means you won't need quite as much dreaming sleep that night because it's believed dreaming does the same sort of consolidating. And that leaves more time for deep, restorative sleep – the type that boosts your immune system, repairs cells and generally acts as 'beauty sleep'.

System Efficiency

Finally, if you don't get up and move around every 90 minutes or so, it has a hugely detrimental effect on all your body's systems. Humans are designed to exert and stretch. Your circulation, nourishment, excretion, mood, muscle and mental tension all depend on body movement to stay in balance. Plus, there's plenty of good research to show that regular movement improves concentration and productivity. Just a few flights of stairs or a walk around the block will make all the difference to your stamina through the working day.

And for all of you out there who are programmed to siesta around 2 every afternoon, I recommend a 2-step rest phase. Find a quiet space and spend 10–15 minutes sitting upright, eyes closed, purely focussing on your breathing (or using any of the techniques from the last chapter). Slowly bring yourself around – *then* take a walk. You'll be amazed at the rejuvenating power of a little meditation followed by activity.

If you tend to be glued to the chair all day, eating lunch as you finish that report, try changing your working patterns to gain the benefits of synchronising with your ultradian rhythms. The most important thing is to become aware of when your brain slows down and your body slumps a little. Practise noticing when you feel sprightly and plough through work super fast. What times during the day does this generally happen? And when does that 'up' phase end? To help you do this, and to remind you to take breaks, try these ideas:

- Set your watch or outlook diary to beep at you every 90 minutes
- Change your screen saver to 'Take 5' or 'You deserve a break'
- Make a pact with a work mate that you'll stop work at a certain time and have a walk together
- Better still, bring back coffee break time in your department. One consultancy team I worked with started doing this and found it significantly strengthened relationships and teamwork (you'll be drinking herbal tea, of course)
- Agree break times at the start of a meeting to ensure it doesn't end up a gruelling marathon
- If you don't work in an office or by a computer, you can still set an alarm to remind you to take a break, make it a habit to phone a loved one at a certain time during the day, or down tools and just do some pleasure reading for a short while.

Answer these questions here or download a clean copy from **www.stop-making-excuses.com**.

How will you remind yourself to take breaks?

✍ ....

....

What will you do to revitalise yourself on these breaks? Make it irresistible! (go back to the pin-up 'Instant Revitalisation' in Chapter 3 – The four energies).

✍ ....

....

How will you stop yourself feeling guilty about not working for a few minutes? If you need permission, then you've got it – from me.

✍ ....

....

EMOTIONAL ENERGY

We've looked at your mental and physical energies. Now I want you to turn your attention to your **EMOTIONAL ENERGY**. Chapters 20–22 will hopefully raise your awareness and shift any habits that are bringing this aspect of your energy down. The bottom line is that we are emotional creatures, and if we don't express our emotions – both positive and negative emotions, it's a big energy drainer. Remember the 'Energy Vessel' from **Chapter 4 – Energy sources and sappers**? Energy 'leakage' is in the form of negative emotions. If we don't express positive emotions for fear of being laughed at or being 'uncool', that's a form of energy leakage, too.

Think about the character of Spock in 'Star Trek'. He's able to be highly effective and logical because he doesn't have emotions to cloud his thinking. Effective, yes, but a pretty flat-line existence.

I want this section to help you have the energy-giving relationships you deserve, both with yourself and others. Imagine starting to operate out of love in all your relationships, even in the ones you think are hopeless sources of pain and negativity. What have you got to lose?

> *We were given magnificent 'birth gifts' – talents, capacities, privileges, intelligences, opportunities – that would remain largely unopened except through our own decision and effort.*

STEPHEN COVEY, *THE 8TH HABIT*

> *I have my faults, but being wrong isn't one of them.*

JIMMY HOFFA (1913–1975?), INFLUENTIAL UNION LEADER IN AMERICA, CONVICTED OF BRIBERY, SERVED 10 YEARS IN PRISON, DISAPPEARED MYSTERIOUSLY AND PRESUMED DEAD

CHAPTER 20

Know yourself

If you want to have the emotional energy that comes from positive relationships (that are happy, loving, 'liking', or mutual goal seeking), then you might have to get to know *yourself* better, first. That's because we all have blind spots when it comes to communicating and building trust. I'm sure you know people who have major blind spots – the ones who seem to have no idea how much they offend, or bore, or sound vain. And then there are the lonely ones who are always trying too hard. They can't see that if they relaxed and lightened up, they'd attract friends easily.

When it comes to ourselves, though, we've lived with our communication style for so long that we can't view it objectively. Have a look at the following list of common issues in relationships, and see if any of them might be something you need to work on:

- Not listening – just waiting for your turn to talk
- Only interested in yourself and your world
- Needy – always looking for a sympathetic ear
- Lack of awareness or anticipation of other's needs
- Lack of honesty
- Unable to ask for what you want or need
- Not being yourself – creating a façade

- Being critical, sniping, using veiled barbs
- Being controlling or manipulative
- Using guilt to get your way
- Using tears or sadness to get your way
- Using aggression to get your way
- Using 'passive aggression', for example refusing to speak to someone or withholding information
- Being a victim
- Being negative or a 'moaning Minnie'
- Being a 'know-it-all'
- Being competitive and constantly comparing
- Only in touch when you need something
- Taking stress or grumpiness out on others
- Being moody, sulky or unpredictable
- Not being appreciative
- Trying too hard to be liked, or funny.

Nobody's perfect, so it's okay to recognise some of these in yourself. If you don't recognise any of them, take a deep breath and look through the list again. If any of the relationships in your life are draining you or stressing you out, then I have to be straight with you and tell you that you're probably resorting to at least one of the above. One exception might be where you are in a relentless caring role, and although you are putting on a brave face, you're feeling resentful or just plain worn out. But those emotions tend to lead to resorting to one of the above, anyway. Whatever the reason for them, they're doing damage to your relationships, and decreasing your emotional energy bank, so it's worth increasing your awareness and growing out of them.

'How do you do that?' you might ask

Well, there's no one, correct way to increase awareness and gain maturity. Paying attention to your behaviour is the main thing, then having planned strategies for when you sense yourself behaving in ways that aren't your best, mature self. It's a case of deciding that you're going to grow up and deal with things in a more effective manner. In the heat of the moment it can be so difficult, but, like going to the gym when you're tired, you always feel better afterward.

I can't hope to cover them all in this book, but here are some strategies you could think about if you're trying to optimise your relationships:

- Always think of asking people about their world, interests, needs and state of health before you blurt out your own. You can disregard this when you have big, big news. But still remember to ask about them afterward . . .
- Just be totally honest, you'll have less to remember (I borrowed this one from Mark Twain)
- In a close personal relationship, agree how you will give each other feedback when things go wrong
- When you want something, ask for it sincerely and nicely, not sarcastically. Or negotiate for it properly, like an adult. That means seeking a mutually agreeable, 'win-win' solution
- When you're with someone, think, 'is being with me brightening their day?', or in the case of a working or teaching relationship, 'is being with me enriching this person?'
- If someone is showing signs of anger or annoyance, but claims nothing is wrong, then calmly and lovingly point out that their words and their body language are not matching at the moment, and invite them to be honest with you
- In sticky situations, pretend the person you respect most in the world is observing you
- In any confrontation, decide from the outset that you will be the reasonable one, and that reason will win the day.

You can download a clean copy of these questions from **www.stop-making-excuses.com**.

What one relationship habit do you have that you need to break?

✍ ....

....

How will you work on this consistently, until it is no longer an issue?

✍ ....

....

Seeking feedback

One great way to get to know yourself better is to regularly seek feedback from colleagues, friends and loved ones. Asking questions such as:

- 'Did you feel supported during this time?'
- 'How can I best help you?'
- 'Do you feel listened to?'
- 'How could we work together more collaboratively?'

needn't be formal or scary. The more you engage people in this way, the more it will feel comfortable to you and those you interact with.

If you're up for it, ask your partner, children and closest friends to answer the following questions about you. A warning here: don't do this unless you're willing to hear the answers, whatever they may be. To approach loved ones with this unusual request, you could say something like:

'I'm working on increasing my energy levels, and as part of that I'm asking the people closest to me to help me learn more about myself. Then I can understand where I might be leaking energy, and where I can strengthen relationships. Would you be willing to answer some questions about me, honestly?' Sure, this is a bit scary, but the answers you get might help you to build better relationships throughout your whole life.

You can download a clean copy from **www.stop-making-excuses.com**.

What are my best traits?

✍...

....

What's a trait I have that you find challenging and why?

✍...

....

Who am I at my best?

✍...

....

Who am I at my worst?

✍...

....

What do I moan about?

✍...

....

What do I praise?

✍...

....

What's the best thing about being my friend/partner/child?

✍...

....

What's the worst thing?

✍...

....

Good luck with this exercise, if you choose to do it. In the next chapter you'll be the one doing the evaluating, as you assess your relationships to find out which ones are giving you energy, and which ones are draining you.

> *In every relationship, in every moment, we teach either love or fear.*

MARIANNE WILLIAMSON, LECTURER IN SPIRITUALITY AND METAPHYSICS, AUTHOR OF BESTSELLING *A RETURN TO LOVE*

> *She's my best friend. She thinks I'm too thin and I think she's a natural blonde.*

CARRIE SNOW, COMEDIAN

CHAPTER 21

Energy-giving relationships

As I said in Chapter 3, some people light up a room when they walk in . . . and some people light up a room when they walk out. Some people are energising to be around – others just the opposite. In fact, every relationship you have results in a net emotional energy gain for you, a net emotional energy loss for you, or neutrality (energy given = energy gained).

If you really want high levels of emotional energy, you need to be careful about what your relationships give you. You may need to change or even eliminate relationships if they consistently drain you. I'm not saying you should sell your mother-in-law, or give your children up for adoption. There are some relationships that will always be more giving than taking (such as parenting, caring for relatives, certain friendships), and that's fine when we enter into them with love and they fulfil us. What I mean is that sometimes we let people lean on us, complain, criticise or ask for favour after favour without ever drawing boundary lines. It's incredibly energy-draining, and I've seen people become ill as a result.

One of the most important things I ever learned about emotions and emotional energy is this: 'We teach people how to treat us'. Dr Phil McGraw writes about this in his inspiring book, *Life Strategies*. He explains that no matter what people are doing to us, we play a role in showing them whether it's okay. If someone isn't appreciating what you're doing for them, never giving you recognition, not respecting you in some way or never showing affection, think about whether they are being rewarded or punished for that behaviour. If you don't communicate how you're feeling, then you are at fault, too.

Just bad luck?

Once I had a client who was stressed out because she felt completely unsupported by her boss. She was asked to work on projects and then left for weeks without mention of them, and she was given responsibilities that she worried were out of her depth. It turned out that she'd had three unsupportive bosses in a row. Bad luck, eh? No, for this lady it was to do with her own lack of communication about what she needed in order to do her job well – more contact, coaching and skills training. Of course her three bosses could have and should have seen what was happening, but in their own busy-ness, they didn't. Fortunately, this lady got the picture pretty quickly, and started communicating very clearly and assertively. And then, lo and behold, she got the support she wanted.

You may or may not be old enough to remember a sitcom called 'All in the Family' (originally aired in the UK as 'Till Death Do Us Part' with Alf Garnett). In the show Edith Bunker is married to Archie, and she waits on him hand and foot. He tells her she's an idiot and she doesn't challenge him. Her self-esteem is so low she's pretty helpless as a person and looks to Archie to tell her what to do. The viewer can see how she only needs to stand up to him, and she finally does this at the end of the final series. Amazingly, he looks completely dumbfounded when she does, and backs down. In an instant he learns that treating her in this way will no longer be acceptable. I know it's only fiction, but it's fiction with a lot of insight into the human condition.

If there are relationships in your life that are all give and no get, you might need to do what Edith did. Calmly and sincerely explain that you won't be spoken to like that, that you feel underappreciated, that you deserve a promotion or you want things to change in some way. You need to be clear about what you don't want, but also what you *do* want. Clear communication is critical in ensuring that your relationships, wherever possible, aren't in a negative energy balance.

If you want great relationships in all areas of your life, the following are some 'first principles' of happy relationships. Have a look at the list and see if there's anything you need to work on. The following list is also a 'pin-up' that you can print out from **www.stop-making-excuses.com**.

> *Shower the people you love with love.*
> JAMES TAYLOR

LIVE WITH ENERGY PIN-UP

The Secrets of Happy Relationships

- Listen and speak in proportion to the number of ears and mouths you have.
- Spend time on relationship-building. Relationships are like house-plants. Without continual watering and feeding, they wither and die.
- When you do something for your partner, friend or relative, do it out of love or not at all. Don't do it if it's to get something (even praise) in return.
- When you do something for a colleague, do it for your own professional development, or for the good of the company, or just out of love (or like) for the individual – not for something in return (apart from your pay cheque, of course). And don't do it out of guilt or fear of losing your job. The only thing that comes of that is stress.
- Never pass up an opportunity to compliment someone.
- Never pass up an opportunity to tell someone how you feel about them, or to give a hug.

- Assume the best intentions. We are often too ready to assume that someone is acting out of spite or dislike, when it's far more likely to be oversight or nothing at all. Always assuming the best intentions, and seeking clarification when you're feeling uncomfortable will minimise misunderstanding, pain and anger. Developing this relationship habit requires a high level of maturity, but it will return to you a more trusting and tight-knit relationship.

- Praise, praise, praise and never criticise. Criticism just doesn't work if you want an energy-giving relationship. Remember that in a relationship you're on the same team. To get the most from your team mates, you praise their strengths enthusiastically and encourage any weak spots to build their confidence. So tell your partner every day how much you appreciate that ride home from work, the cup of tea in the morning, or how she ironed your shirt. Thank your kids for helping with the housework. Thank your colleagues for their support. Do this *even if you think they don't do enough!* The more you praise something, the more people will do it. The more they feel criticised, the less inclined they are to change. This is absolutely true, and if you don't believe me, just try it!

- When you need or want something, ask for it. Ask kindly and sincerely and you'll likely get it. Not only that, you make it okay for the other person to ask for things in the same way. In the case of your needs not being met, or wanting someone to do something in a different way, this is *very different to criticism*. For example, you could say, 'I always seem to do all the washing and ironing. Why can't you help me more?' OR, you could say, 'Darling, would you help me with the washing and ironing today? I would so appreciate it.' (with no sarcasm in your voice – otherwise it's just as bad as 'Why can't you . . .').

- Be brave about difficult conversations. You might need to have a more in-depth conversation about sharing the household chores, or whatever. A good opener in difficult conversations is 'I am feeling that . . .', or 'When you ____, I feel ____, and what I would really like is ____.'

Don't say 'You make me feel . . .' because that's not true. They are just behaving – you're choosing how to feel about it. If the other person is uncooperative, or refuses to discuss the matter, explain that this is important to you, and you'd like to find a way forward that makes you both happy.

* Be prepared to either walk away if your needs aren't met – or – if the relationship is with a relative, find a way to accept the level of relationship you're getting without letting it ruin your life.

For lots more good stuff on how to improve your relationships, see the resource list at the end of this book.

How to 'win' an argument

Did you ever get into an argument and find yourself shouting 'Listen to me!', and the answer came back 'No, you listen to me!' It's natural to think this way in the middle of conflict, but it's not the greatest way to create understanding and trust. Try: 'Let me listen to your side of the story' – then do just that until the person is all talked-out. After that, they just might be in the right frame of mind to listen to your side. Only then can you begin to work through a solution that is agreeable to both of you.

To increase the number of energy-giving relationships you have, try the following worksheet. You can download a clean copy from **www.stop-making-excuses.com**.

What relationships in your life are currently draining you?

✍..

....

....

What do think the real underlying causes of this are?

Consider: Is the person unhappy, distressed, distracted, envious, jealous? Are you allowing it? Letting a pattern develop? Not giving the relationship the time and attention it needs? Could it be that your anger or disappointment is leaking out?

✍..

....

....

What strategies will you use to improve the relationship?

Look back over this chapter for ideas. If you're afraid to do anything, consider this: What have you got to lose?

✍..

....

....

When will you take action on this?

If there's a conversation you need to have, or new way of behaving you must cultivate, in order to have higher energy levels, why delay? Remember that you can blame others for your misery all you like, but it won't

make you any happier. Put something in your diary now, before the desire
to change passes.

✍ ....

....

....

❝ *What do you think is the number one trait people unconsciously admire in others?
First and foremost, they are drawn towards individuals who look healthy and
vital – people who are putting out energy into the room rather than those who are
sucking it in. If there's one thing that suggests health and vitality, it's positive energy,
which can be projected in the way you come into a room.* ❞
NICHOLAS BOOTHAM, *HOW TO CONNECT IN BUSINESS*

“ *I have learned from experience that the greater part of our happiness or misery depends on our dispositions and not on our circumstances.* **”**

MARTHA WASHINGTON, AMERICA'S FIRST FIRST LADY

“ *Start every day off with a smile and get it over with.* **”**

W. C. FIELDS

CHAPTER 22

Happiness is a journey, not a destination

I wonder if you're ever guilty of putting off being happy, feeling good or enjoying yourself until you've completed a certain chore, worked a certain number of hours, got the promotion or finished the degree? It's easily done given a culture of reward for achievement, praise for tasks completed – like we're not allowed to have fun along the way because otherwise, why would there be a prize for enduring it? Besides, in some organisations, schools and families, it's a bit uncool to be enjoying your work.

Despite all this, you can enjoy the journey of your life, even if you have loads of work to do or life is a bit tough right now. And ***if you can find more ways to be happy on your journey, I guarantee you'll have more energy and vitality***.

In her book *The Emotional Energy Factor*, Mira Kirshenbaum tells the story of growing up a poor immigrant in New York City. She makes the point that in the midst of poverty and misery, there were those who smiled and joked and lived happily anyway. One of my own mottos for life is that 'I'm happy anyway'. I know bad stuff happens in the world, but I choose to focus on my many blessings and all the beautiful things around me.

> **❝** *I don't think of all the misery, but of the beauty that remains.* **❞**
> HELEN KELLER, AMERICAN AUTHOR, ACTIVIST AND LECTURER

Where does happiness come from anyway? Studies reveal that it mostly comes from being loved, loving others, having a purpose, a sense of belonging and feeling valued by family, work or society.

Some people grow up thinking that their worth and their source of happiness is about what they do, not about who they are. So I want you to think about where your happiness comes from, and whether you:

(a) are happy as a rule, but with some upsets, prompting you to restore equilibrium or

(b) are relatively unhappy as a rule but get happy when certain events occur.

In other words, is your happiness a result of your attitude to life, and finding joy along the road, or is it linked to circumstances?

Remember Sue from **Chapter 16 – Eat, drink and be energised**? She radically changed her diet (and the food she truly loves) as a result of having cancer and deciding to look after her body. When I interviewed her for the book she also talked about how she has put enjoyment back into her life, as opposed to just trying to get all the chores done. She said, 'I was always thinking about past and future. Rather than worrying when I wake up, or speculating about the

> *We act as though comfort and luxury were the chief requirements of life, when all that we need to make us happy is something to be enthusiastic about.*
> ALBERT EINSTEIN

future, I think, what would I like to do today? And I include at least some things that I enjoy each day. I think about "now"!'

Answer the following questions to help you discover how you can make the journey of your life even happier – consistently!

First, let's explore any current habits that might be reducing the fun of the ride. We all have at least one of these, maybe more. Look at the following list to identify which of these apply, then circle your answers here or download a clean copy from **www.stop-making-excuses.com**.

- Holding onto negative emotions for too long – for example, when they aren't serving any positive solution focus or when it's time to let go and move on
- Resenting any chores you have to do before you get to the 'good stuff'
- Only showing your sense of humour when you are officially 'doing something fun'
- Needing things to be done a certain way for you to feel comfortable and happy
- Using phrases such as 'I'll be happy when . . . '
- Thinking that a promotion, new house, new car, new relationship will make you happy or solve your problems
- Waiting till an event passes to be able to relax

- Needing to feel in control of other peoples' reactions
- Unable to feel happy or content when those around you aren't

(I'm not suggesting you whistle through a crisis – just be aware of whether you're taking on too much of someone else's 'stuff' – their tension, sadness, anger or other negative emotions)

Reviewing what you've circled, describe a typical or recurring situation where these things happen:

✎ ....

....

What could you do and feel instead to feel happier?

Bear in mind your long-term happiness. For instance, will avoiding conflict help you let go of something that isn't really that important? Or will avoiding it only cause stress, making it even harder to finally tackle the issue calmly?

✎ ....

....

When you wake up, what's normally your first thought?

Joy in greeting the new day?

Focus on your body waking up and energising?

Schedules, to-do's, chores?

Dreading something?

Feeling exhausted?

Where's my double espresso?

✎ ....

....

If you think about things that aren't serving your vitality, what will you focus on instead and how will you shift that focus?

✎ ....

....

How do you approach chores?

Prioritise and accept you can't do everything?

Think 'the sooner I start, the sooner I'll finish'?

Think 'How can I make this fun?'

See them as part of life?

As a necessary evil? Or just plain evil!

Do you ask for help, share them and use teamwork?

Or do you become a martyr?

....

....

How can you be happier when doing chores?

....

....

Are you prone to taking offence to comments from colleagues or family members?

If so, why do you think this is? Be honest ... do you crave the drama? Need the attention? Sympathy? Do you lack the confidence in yourself and assume people think the worst of you?

....

....

How can you find the confidence to assume the best intentions in those moments? Or ask (calmly) for clarification?

....

....

Have you had a bereavement or tragedy in your life that continues to impede your happiness after a reasonable period of time?

'Reasonable' is individual, but in your heart of hearts you will know how long this is.

....

....

What do you need to do to let go and move on?

Suggestions: seek counselling, cognitive behavioural therapy, have a 'letting go' ceremony of some sort, see yourself in a new light, choose a date to emerge as your new dynamic self.

✎ ....

....

Are you holding a grudge or failing to forgive someone?

It's hard to be 100% happy and energised if you're holding onto anger. What good is it doing you? Could you just let go of it? If you don't think you can, what would you have to do to be able to let go? If your answer is to do with justice or seeing another pay for an injustice, remember that:

a) you can still seek justice in some way without holding onto destructive anger

b) if you never get 'justice', will you carry your anger to your grave?

✎ ....

....

When faced with a setback, how long does it take you to restore equilibrium? How can you begin to focus on the positive more quickly after these setbacks? How can you be happier anyway?

✎ ....

....

What one thing will you add into your life that will give you sheer pleasure, fun and happiness?

✎ ....

....

Sarah, 32, was so stressed and unhappy when I first met her that I don't know how she was holding it together at work. I guess like many people, her life outside work was falling apart, but she was somehow keeping a professional demeanour during her working day.

She told me though, that she absolutely loathed her job as a solicitor. All of her peers were gunning for partner, but she said she just didn't care about that. She hated the thought of working her butt off to make partner, only to face even more pressure and long hours than she did now. The hours and fatigue were destroying her long-term partnership, and she was starting to wonder if she'd ever have a family. The obvious question to ask her then, was, 'Why don't you change jobs?'

'Because I can't afford to.'

'Come again?'

'Well, my partner and I have taken on a big mortgage, and to be honest, I wouldn't want to have to curb my lifestyle. I'm very comfortably off, and we have some fantastic holidays.'

'I thought you said you were miserable.'

'Well yes, but,'

'But what?'

'I feel so confused.' And then the floodgates opened. I saw that the pressure of living out of line with what she really valued was causing excruciating pain. When she had let it all out, I had to ask the next question.

'So, what will you do to be happy again?'

'That's a good question.'

We explored this whole idea over a few sessions, and Sarah saw that although she had this vague idea that career progression was a means to an end (happiness, that is, and financial security), the journey was killing her. She needed to find a way to live that would make her happy on the way. In the end she didn't change careers. She really did enjoy law, so she changed firms to a small, local establishment where partnership wouldn't mean six-figure bonuses, but where she does have a life outside of work. And if she does decide to start a family, she'll be able to maintain a work–life balance.

At one point she said to me, 'I've wasted so much time' and I suggested that perhaps it wasn't a waste at all. It was an important lesson in her life that she needed in order to move forward to a happier life.

SPIRIT ENERGY

There is an ultimate source of energy which is available to you all the time: when everything in your life is hunky-dory, and when it seems things couldn't be worse. It's your SPIRIT ENERGY, and it will never fail you if you choose to accept its amazing power. But, like mental, physical and emotional energies, having this energy is a result of the choices **you** make. In the case of spirit energy, the choices have to do with:

- whether you find joy in life
- whether you live what you value (walk your talk)
- whether you have a reason for hanging around on this planet
- learning the lessons that life gives you.

We've already covered values and how you'll live them, and just talked about happiness in the last chapter. So the next two chapters are about the second two aspects of how you can tap into this awesome energy.

If you're thinking, 'well, I'm not sure this stuff is really for me', can I persuade you to take the time to go through these two short chapters? I think you might find some compelling reasons here to live your life to the max and get rid of your justifications.

" *There is for each man, perfect self-expression. There is a place which he is to fill and no one else can fill, something which he is to do, which no one else can do; it is his destiny!* "

FLORENCE SCOVEL-SHINN (1871–1940), SPIRITUAL TEACHER, HEALER AND AUTHOR OF BESTSELLING *THE GAME OF LIFE AND HOW TO PLAY IT*

" *Life is like a sewer. What you get out of it depends on what you put in.* "

TOM LEHRER, SATIRIST AND HARVARD LECTURER

CHAPTER 23

Get a life!

I don't know about you, but for me the quickest way to get demoralised is to feel that I'm working my guts out only to get through my in-tray – like there's no forward motion in any particular direction. Given the demands of career, the endless administration of a household, parenting or caring for relatives, it's easy to feel this way.

However, a natural human need is to develop, create, and strive for things. When we don't do any of that for an extended period of time, we can get stale, lethargic and resentful – in other words, lose energy.

Consider the example I gave in **Chapter 3 – The four energies** of ticking all the boxes for health and relationships, but feeling bored at work and no sense of going anywhere. Have you ever been there? Are you there now? If you feel:

* Stuck
* Resentful about your work
* Knowing you should move on, but unsure about what to do next
* Like you're on a treadmill and you just have to keep going

then a lack of **spirit energy** may be the problem, be it lack of direction, no connection to values or just no joy.

The proactive life

I was being interviewed on BBC Merseyside about two weeks ago, discussing stress in the workplace. The presenter said, 'Let's face it, most people can't change their jobs.' How wrong that is! You can change your job or your *whole life*. It might take some planning and effort, but you (yes, you) can get to a place where you're doing what you love, and enjoying the journey of life. The energy drain of hating your job or some other major aspect of life is horrendous. Luckily, I haven't spent too much time in that position. If that's where you are now, then in Chapters 25–27 you can get going planning your new life.

The point is, if you have a compelling reason to get up in the morning, something that lights your fire, you're going to feel more fuelled and jazzed. So, what is it about a sense of purpose that gives energy? First let me say that you do not have to have omniscience about what you're supposed to be doing with your life. One of my clients recently said to me, 'I don't know what my purpose is, but living in line with my values gives me a sense of worth and contribution. I'm also getting a kick out of the challenge of my job right now, and that keeps me going when I'm feeling a little tired or discouraged about something.' This guy is living proactively, he's happy, and he is determined to make a success of his small business.

> ❝ Life if not tried, it is simply survived, if you're standing outside the fire. ❞
> GARTH BROOKES

Here are some reasons that living proactively gives you energy:

- We naturally work toward goals and deadlines. If we identify with the goals, we're motivated. Motivation is an amazing energiser – just ask any parent or teacher. If we don't identify with goals, we aren't motivated and lose energy

- Feeling we're doing something worthwhile is always given as one of the top three reasons people stay in jobs. We stay where we're happy and feel fulfilled because it's energising
- When we live proactively we feel in control, and a sense of control brings resilience and energy.

> *We are all in the gutter, but some of us are looking at the stars.*
> OSCAR WILDE

If you're working toward something, anything, it will give you amazing resilience to pressure. A recent workshop delegate said to me, 'In my previous job, the company was winding down, and the last six months were just so demoralising. We were doing the same work with the same clients, but we knew we just weren't headed anywhere. To be honest, I started to feel really awful coming into work. Even with the pressures of this job, it's much better than feeling like I'm drifting, doing nothing.'

Recreation

Another important element of 'having a life' is having recreation. Note the origin of this word: it's about renewal, rebirth. Hobbies and interests reinvigorate our minds, create a seedbed for creative ideas and make us interesting as people – which enriches relationships. Playtime is vital – have you all but stopped doing it because you're just so 'busy'?

Part of an energised life is having fun, trying new things, having memorable experiences outside of your normal routine. It's an awesome way to cultivate spirit energy!

Workaholic and happy?

In my 18 years in energy management, I've only met one person who I truly believe is happy devoting practically his entire waking existence to work. The HR department of his company phoned me and said, 'We have a fairly new employee we'd like you to see. Since he started, all he does is work. He's the first in, last to leave, comes in on weekends, works through lunch. Quite frankly, we're worried he's going to have a heart attack or something.' So I saw him. He couldn't understand what the issue was. He said he just really enjoys working and getting things done, and he has no interest whatsoever in having hobbies or recreation outside of work. This is extreme, I know, but the guy is happy with his life. This isn't the path to happiness for the vast majority of us, but who can say that he's wrong? The key is to pay attention to how you're spending your precious time so that you don't get to the end of your life and think, 'What was I thinking of, spending my whole life on the treadmill?'

A perfect diamond

Finally, I've got one more thing to remind you of on the subject of 'having a life', and it is: ***Don't be afraid to be you*** – the real magnificent you. It's terribly draining to wear a mask, to try to be someone you're not. If you want energy, be the natural 'you'. If some people don't like it – tough! Not everyone in this world is going to like you, so you may as well be liked by people you're going to like back. How's that for some deep philosophy?

Here's an analogy that might help you if you struggle with revealing the real, wonderful you. I have read and heard about it from a number of sources, and whenever I explain it to anyone, they instantly see that it describes them. It goes like this:

Each of us is born a magnificent, perfect diamond. We sparkle, shine and radiate energy. But, since not everyone in this world operates out of love, we encounter things like criticism, envy, jealousy and bullying. Those behaviours toward us, and our own egotistical responses, shovel horse manure onto our beautiful diamond. We collect piles of horse manure until you can't even see the diamond anymore. But we don't want to show the horse manure to the world, because that is too painful. So we paint nail varnish (of different varieties and colours) over the top of the manure. This is the façade we show the world, which pales in comparison to the precious gem that lies beneath.

> *We must overcome the notion that we must be regular . . . it robs you of the chance to be extraordinary and leads you to the mediocre.*
> UTA HAGEN

What can you do with that analogy? Well, perhaps you could be more aware of when you feel too afraid to let the real you shine, and talk yourself into giving everyone around you a chance to glimpse the diamond. Marianne Williamson, in her amazing book *A Return to Love*, says this:

'. . . our deepest fear is not that we are inadequate. Our deepest fear is that we are powerful beyond measure. It is our light, not our darkness, that most frightens us. We ask ourselves, Who am I to be brilliant, gorgeous, talented, fabulous? Actually, who are you *not* to be?'

If you fear that others will laugh at you, think you're stupid or won't accept you, then make the above quote into a poster, stick it on your 'fridge, and read it every day for the next six weeks at least.

You don't have to be an Einstein or a Ghandi to display the full power of your diamond. You might make a small, loving contribution to charity or alleviate one person's suffering. You might simply raise a family in love. That might be all you need to do to tap into your spirit energy.

> *I don't have much here, really, there are no luxuries – just a few CDs and the odd photo scattered around. But I'm so lucky because the pleasure is inside me, the luxuries are inside me. Those moments shared with friends and loved ones, the simple things that make people smile – they're with me all the time. They're priceless and, luckily for my endeavour, weightless, too!*
> ELLEN MACARTHUR, *RACE AGAINST TIME* – THE STORY OF ELLEN'S RECORD-BREAKING SOLO SAIL AROUND THE WORLD IN 2005

" *The purpose of life, after all, is to live it, to taste experience to the utmost, to reach out eagerly and without fear for newer and richer experiences.* "

ELEANOR ROOSEVELT

" *Three little sentences will get you through life. Number one: Cover for me. Number two: Oh, good idea, boss. Number three: It was like that when I got here.* "

HOMER SIMPSON

CHAPTER 24

Learn your life lessons

In this chapter I'm going to try to tell you about some lessons in life that I've learned, some the hard way. If you don't know about them, they can cause energy haemorrhages. Learning them will increase your wisdom and in turn, your spirit energy. I want to start with a newspaper clipping I saw stuck on the refrigerator of one of my mom's dear friends, about 10 years ago. I'm not sure how long it had been there, but suffice to say the following bit of prose has been around a long time.

Ten Rules for Living – author unknown

1. You will receive a body. You may like it or hate it, but it's yours to keep for the entire period.
2. You will learn lessons. You are enrolled in a full-time informal school called 'life'.
3. There are no mistakes – only lessons. Growth is a process of trial, error and experimentation. The 'failed' experiments are as much a part of the process as the experiments the ultimately 'work'.
4. Lessons are repeated until they are learned. A lesson will be presented to you in various forms until you have learned it. When you have learned it, you can go on to the next lesson.

5. Learning lessons does not end. There's no part of life that doesn't contain lessons.

6. If you delay happiness until you have learned the current lesson, or come through a difficult period in your life, or got the promotion, or finished the project, then you will wait a long time for happiness.

7. What you make of your life is up to you. You have all the tools and resources you need.

8. The attitude you have to life is the single most important factor in determining whether your life will be happy or sad.

9. The answers to life's questions are inside of you. All you need to do is look, listen and trust.

10. You will forget all of this.

I love this list because it contains so many life lessons that I've found to be absolutely true in my life. Everyone I show this to says the same.

Groundhog Day

The idea that you get the same lesson over and over until you learn it is an interesting one. Remember my example earlier in **Chapter 21 – Energy-giving relationships** of the lady who had three unsupportive bosses in a row? She had to learn to be assertive, and that we teach people how to treat us. I have a friend who always seems to end up with needy men; another who is always in debt. It's usually the tougher lessons that we don't learn first time around. The key is to be big enough to admit the part you play in your own problems, and make the firm decision to change.

> " *Desire creates the power.* "
> RAYMOND HOLLINGWELL

Everything you need

Another key lesson from Ten Rules for Living is that you already have everything you need to have everything you desire. I'm not going to pretend that you don't need any new skills or help from anyone. But basically, you have the ability to do anything you want. If you don't believe it, then of course you'll never realise the power you have.

> *You can have anything you want if you want it badly enough. You can be anything you want to be, do anything you set out to accomplish if you hold to that desire with singleness of purpose.*
> ABRAHAM LINCOLN

Stop struggling

Do you know people for whom life is such a struggle? They're always late, rushed, stressed, harassed by their kids, mother-in-law, whatever. My advice on this is to simply stop struggling. It's a black hole of energy consumption. Your energy. There may be things you need to let go of worrying about, let go of feeling hurt about, or simply cut out of your life so that you're not so overcommitted.

You might also need to accept the way things are in the world. I'm not saying don't stand up for what you believe, I'm saying that you might have to accept things like traffic, late trains and the way certain people behave – if you want to stop being drained of energy by them.

Never stop learning and growing

One of the reasons I believe my grandfather lived to be 95 was that he never let a day go by without learning something. He was a big reader, curious about an endless number of subjects, and always looking forward to the next project. Personal development gives you energy, and that kind of energy can literally be a life force. You only have to look at post-retirement mortality statistics to see this. A recent study published in the *British Journal of Medicine* showed an increased risk of death for those who retire at 55 vs those who retire at 65. I personally don't think it's about doing paid work or not. I think it's about

> *Anyone who stops learning is old, whether at twenty or eighty. Anyone who keeps learning stays young. The greatest thing in life is to keep your mind young.*
> HENRY FORD

Don't go through life, grow through life.
ERIC BUTTERWORTH

having a reason to get out of bed, whether it's to study, do charitable work or look after your grandchildren.

Take a little step toward wisdom by answering these questions about some important life lessons. You can download a clean copy from **www.stop-making-excuses.com**.

Can you identify any patterns of frustration, anger or pain that you might have something to learn from? And what do you think the learning might be?

....

....

What things have you ruled out in your life because 'they're just not possible for you'?

You flippant lot, I don't mean finding out you're actually royalty, or that a distant uncle died and left you £1,000,000.

....

....

Of those things, which ones would you secretly love to achieve?

....

....

What one thing will you do toward making that dream a reality?

....

....

When will you do this one thing?

You don't think I'd let you off this question, do you?

....

....

PART IV

Action plans you actually take action on

> *The difference between one man and another is not mere ability. It is energy.*
>
> THOMAS ARNOLD (1795–1842), HISTORIAN AND
> INFLUENTIAL HEADMASTER OF RUGBY SCHOOL

> *You can't expect to hit the jackpot if you don't put a few nickels in the machine.*
>
> FLIP WILSON, COMEDIAN

CHAPTER 25

Filling your vitality vessel

N ow it's over to you to think about what your formula is for keeping your Vitality Vessel full. I know it's not going to be brimming over every single day . . . but why not aim for that? People frequently ask me if I really feel so energetic all the time, and the honest answer is that, yes, 99% of the time I feel fantastic, happy and energised. The thing is, you don't get that level of energy for free. You're human (I'm guessing), so you have to work with your human psyche and physiology. Too many of my clients are in denial that they ever need to rest, or need to spend time on their relationships in order to keep them. If you want the vivacity that makes life sheer joy, you've got to have a formula for filling, and re-filling, your vessel. The formula is going to change as you go through life, but to make your demanding life sustainable, you do need a formula, and you have to more or less stick to it!

Below is a simplified version of the Vitality Vessel illustration from **Chapter 4 – Energy sources and sappers**. It's blank for you to fill in your own special, individual, personal, unique recipe for an overflowing bucket. I urge you to look back over the **Vitality Now!** section to remind you of the sorts of things that fill up your vessel. Use Chapter 4's completed questionnaire to remind you of your own current energy sources as well as the *sappers*. Then create your personalised diagram with the energy sources that you already have in place, and others you **actually intend to develop as habits.** Writing down a bunch of stuff you know you'll never do will only make you feel bad and reinforce your past excuses. Also, be honest about the ways in which you leak energy. To figure out solutions to your problems, you need to look them squarely in the face.

The next chapter is all about how you take real steps toward change. No more sitting around lamenting your lack of energy, fitness, weight loss or happiness. Time to do something about it.

As usual, you can download a clean copy of this diagram from **www.stop-making-excuses.com**.

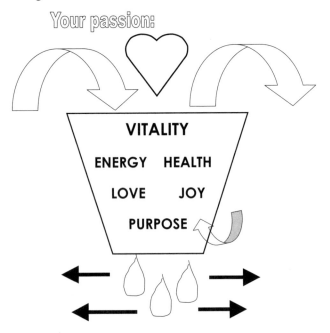

" *Whatever you do, or dream you can do, begin it. Boldness has power, magic and genius in it.* "

JOHANN WOLFGANG GOETHE (1739–1832), GERMAN POET, NOVELIST, DRAMATIST, THEORIST, PAINTER AND NATURAL SCIENTIST

" *God is a DJ, life is a dance floor, love is the rhythm, you are the music . . . so get your ass on the dance floor NOW!* "

PINK

CHAPTER 26

Steps to taking action and LOVING IT!

Any change can be made in a moment if there is enough of a motivation to do it, and a big enough perceived benefit. But some changes may require more 'coaching' and planning before that 'moment' comes. This can be because there are skills required to make the change, the benefits are not clear, or there may be perceived benefits in *not* changing.

As you work through the questions in this chapter, I ask you to be willing to approach things totally differently to how you might have approached them before.

Remember, if you do what you've always done, you'll get what you've always got.

STEP ONE – What do you want?

This was the title of the very first chapter of this book, and a *must* as a starting point. If you aren't clear about what you want, there's little hope you'll get anything. Re-read the first chapter if you need some help thinking about a proactive vs a reactive life. You need to have a clear, detailed and absolutely beautiful picture of what benefits will come to you if you make certain choices. What will it feel like? What will you look like? How will it increase your self-esteem? Your productivity? How will you benefit financially? How will it also benefit others? The visualised outcomes need to be detailed to create an accurate compass for the direction in which you are moving, and they need to be beautiful to get you excited about going there. Take the time to write your answers right here, right now.

✎ ....

....

....

STEP TWO – Make it an imperative!

The second, critical step is **MAKE IT AN IMPERATIVE** to get it. I can't emphasise this enough, because if it is not an imperative, it will always get pushed to the bottom of the priority list and the essential actions to achieve the change will get skipped more often than not.

Ask yourself what the consequences will be if you fail to make this change. What will you miss out on? How regretful will you be and why? Picture yourself in the future not having made this change and what you will have lost. Imagine the pain you might experience (physical or emotional), because this can be a great spur to make you act.

Another powerful way to make a change imperative is by creating a circumstance that will cause embarrassment or financial loss if you don't follow through, or simply leaves you with no other choice. For instance, you could promise your child that you will start running regularly, sign

up for a fun-run and get friends to sponsor you to run the event for a favourite charity. That way, if you don't train, you will break your promise, and seriously suffer on race day. If you don't run in the event, you will have to explain yourself to all the people who sponsored you.

One client of mine who lived in London literally sold his car so that he would have to cycle the five miles to work each day, or face a difficult journey by public transport. He said that he found he didn't really need a car living in the city, he saved enough money for a fabulous holiday, and it also got him to make other short journeys by foot or bike.

So get radical. What will it take to make your change an *imperative?*

STEP THREE – Make a plan

Now you need to make a detailed plan of how to get to your goal. Even the ablest General with the biggest imperative to win a battle makes a plan. A plan keeps you on track, and allows you to check your progress. Sun Tzu, in his famous, ancient text, *The Art of War*, said that time spent planning is never wasted! Set some time aside when you can sit down in peace with your favourite music playing and a nice cup of tea (herbal, of course). Then be imaginative and resourceful, and prepare to commit to some real actions and dates.

" Never mistake motion for action. "
ERNEST HEMINGWAY

Important Elements of a Plan for Change

- A time-line with your goal reached by a deadline
- Detailed steps along the time-line that allow you to check progress
- Resources you need to gather to enable the steps to happen, including the human resource that will help and support you
- Contingency plans for obstacles that may be foreseeable, and 'fat' in the system for those that are not, such as extra time, extra money or resources.

Use the following template to create your own action plan. You can download a clean copy from **www.stop-making-excuses.com**.

STEP FOUR – Repetition

With the elements of change that need to be a regular part of your day or week, such as meditation, exercise, a time management technique or repeating your affirmations, you need to practise them consistently, and have a reminder system that works for you. If you have a great enough imperative, it may serve as your reminder, but most of us need a system to make this new habit squeeze into a busy schedule. Here are some simple ideas for creating repetition that will embed your habit into your life and keep it there:

- Put it into your diary now for every time you will practise this habit for the next six months. Put it in red ink, and pretend it is an appointment with the person you would most like to meet in the world
- Schedule it into Outlook as a recurring appointment that will beep at you
- Pin a note to your bedside table so you see it when you wake up. My daughter, who sleeps in the top of a bunk-bed, simply has a note on her ceiling that says 'GET UP!' That's the 'sensible organise the night before' self telling the morning 'I want to stay in bed' self what to do! Similarly, put a note in a desk drawer you open often, on your refrigerator or by your bathroom mirror

MY IMPERATIVE:

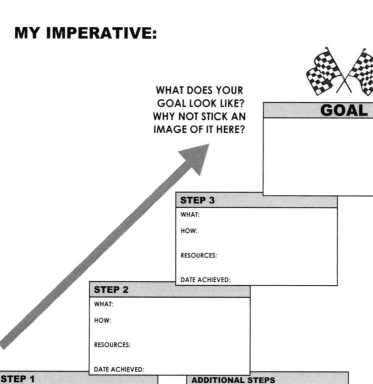

WHAT DOES YOUR
GOAL LOOK LIKE?
WHY NOT STICK AN
IMAGE OF IT HERE?

GOAL

STEP 3
WHAT:
HOW:
RESOURCES:
DATE ACHIEVED:

STEP 2
WHAT:
HOW:
RESOURCES:
DATE ACHIEVED:

STEP 1
WHAT:
HOW:
RESOURCES:
DATE ACHIEVED:

ADDITIONAL STEPS

- Create a screen saver that reminds and motivates you
- Arrange with a friend to phone you on the days you have committed to doing this habit. Tell them they are permitted to get tough with you, and crack the whip if you haven't delivered
- Better still, do the habit with a friend and make appointments to meet together

- Work with a personal trainer or coach who will expect regular reports on your progress
- Agree to pay £1 (or more if you're well-off) to a charity you aren't particularly fond of for every day you don't do this habit. Your friends can check on you
- Make yourself a star-chart, with a reward for when you fill the chart. Sounds silly, but I have clients who have used this to good effect
- Promise yourself a reward if you manage to do the habit regularly for three weeks, then 3 months.

Even the most motivated, saintly health-worshipers need to review on a regular basis whether they are renewing energy in all areas in the best way they can. It is an on-going, lifelong process to keep everything in balance, and consider how things could be even better.

> " It doesn't matter when you start, as long as you start now. "
> W. EDWARDS DENNING

For this step, you need to be honest about what would really work for you. You could:

- have a coaching relationship in which the coach phones you every six months and reviews your vitality goals with you. A switched-on friend could also fill this role
- put it in your diary every 3–6 months to do a vitality audit on yourself, possibly using the vitality questionnaire in this book to check your score
- use New Year's Day each year not to make resolutions, but to renew your great vitality habits.

Unless this step is built in, it is SO easy to drift away from the routines that restore us and keep us at our best.

> " Pearls lie not on the seashore. If thou desirest one thou must dive for it. "
> CHINESE PROVERB

If you need a weekly reminder of the importance of your vitality, sign up for my weekly vitality tips to be sent to you by email. Just go to **www.stop-making-excuses.com** and look for the link to 'vitality tips'. It's free!

How will you create the repetition you need to get your new habits ingrained for life?

✎ ....

....

STEP FIVE – Make it fun!

Change is difficult to sustain when there is no joy in it! Unless you're a masochist, vitality habits need to be fun for you to keep doing them!

How will you make sure you enjoy your new habit(s)?

Don't say it's impossible. Be creative.

✎ ....

....

Dear Me

Back in Chapter 6, I showed you a selection of commitment letters that my workshop delegates have written to themselves. There's one more I want to show you because it is such an inspiration. This guy had a pretty serious rethink of his life on that day, and he wrote this amazing letter to himself:

> *Never be afraid to do something new. Noah was an amateur; the Titanic was built by professionals.*
> JAMES PRENTICE

Dear M, Let's get those negatives out of the way first.

You are not the best at everything!

You will never be the best at everything!

You don't need to be the best at everything!

The trouble with you is it always has to be black and white – if you're not the best at something you won't even accept that you're adequate at it. You seem to believe that things should come easily to you – if you can't pick up new things quickly you want to give up. You don't want to start something unless you can already see the end.

Face it . . .

You are already respected for your skills and experience.

You're not an imposter – you've been here 12 years and consistently get reviews and feedback that tell you you're doing OK.

The person you're competing with is yourself – which is stupid.

You need to let go of things and trust others – maybe they won't make as good a job of it as you would, they may do it better – or maybe that's what you're afraid of!

You need to work at building up some self confidence. Find a technique to practise and go for it!

Make some life style changes . . .

Get your lazy fat arse to the gym . . . no excuses. It may not be the most fun way to exercise but it'll do while you look for something else. It'll improve your self esteem as well as your girth.

Join that night school class – you'll improve your social life and improve your Italian at the same time.

Invite people round more often, the new house is a bit off the beaten track – if you're not careful it'll become a hermitage!

Don't give up the folk club. It may not be the most exciting music in the world but it puts you in the position of having to perform when you know what you're doing isn't perfect – the important thing is that you're taking risks and having a go.

All the best,

M

Time to make your action plan. What are you waiting for?

" Life is either a daring adventure or nothing. "
HELEN KELLER, AMERICAN AUTHOR, ACTIVIST AND LECTURER

" *. . . if we wait for the moment when everything, absolutely everything is ready, we shall never begin.* **"**

IVAN TURGENEV

" *Decide that you want it more than you are afraid of it.* **"**

BILL COSBY

CHAPTER 27

Decision time

I f you're still holding back from committing to a new life of energy-giving habits, then why?

Any change, even change for the better, takes energy. Sometimes the pain of maintaining a bad habit isn't great enough to make us shift to a new, good habit. Could that be the case for you?

The thing is, once you go through the process of change (however difficult that may be), and stick with it, you get the payoff forever.

Could you focus on the payoff, and commit to doing whatever it takes to get it? If you haven't taken any actions yet, then I urge you to go back to Chapters 1, 2 and then 26, because they are what it's all about. What do you want, what do you value, and what are you going to do about it?

> " There are no shortcuts to any place worth going. "
> ANONYMOUS

Recommended resources

MORE ENERGY

The Impact Code by Nigel Risner – **ISBN 1-84112-716-7**

On Form by Jim Loehr and Tony Schwartz – **ISBN 1-85788-325-X**

High Energy Habits by Bill Ford – **ISBN 0-7434-2894-3**

High Energy Living by Robert K. Cooper – **ISBN 1-57954-126-7**

FITNESS

The Corporate Athlete by Jack Groppel – **ISBN 0-471-35369-8**

The Exercise Bible by Joanna Hall – **ISBN 1-85626-555-2**

Fitness for Life Manual by Matt Roberts – **ISBN 0-7513-3866-4**

Exercise for Everyone by Cornel Chin – **ISBN 1-84400-086-9**

Yoga the Iyengar Way by Silva, Mira and Shyam Mehta –
ISBN 0-86318-420-0

The *Gaiam* series of Yoga and Pilates workouts on DVD are excellent. Rodney Yee and Suzanne Deason are especially recommended for clear instructions and great workouts

NUTRITION

The Food Doctor Everyday Diet by Ian Marber –
ISBN 1-4053-0605-X (not just for weight loss)
Easy GI diet by Helen Foster – **ISBN 0-600-61002-0**
Bodyfoods for Busy People by Jane Clarke – **ISBN 1-84400-085-0**
Eat Smart Play Hard by Liz Applegate PhD – **ISBN 1-57954-344-8**
The Food Bible by Judith Wills – **ISBN 1-902757-36-X**
Eating Well for Optimum Health by Dr. Andrew Weil –
ISBN 0-316-85479-4 (for serious study)

SMOKING CESSATION

Allen Carr's Easy Way to Stop Smoking by Allen Carr –
ISBN 0-14-027763-3

EMOTIONAL ENERGY

Working With Emotional Intelligence by Daniel Goleman –
ISBN 0-7475-4384-4
The Emotional Energy Factor by Mira Kirshenbaum –
ISBN 0-385-33609-8
Feel the Fear and Do It Anyway by Susan Jeffers – **ISBN 0-09-974100-8**
Authentic Happiness by Martin E.P. Seligman PhD –
ISBN 0-7432-2298-9

CHALLENGING RELATIONSHIPS

Difficult Conversations by Douglas Stone, Bruce Patton, Sheila Heen –
ISBN 0-14-028852-X
Getting to Yes by Roger Fisher and William Ury –
ISBN 0-14-015735-2
How to Cope with Difficult People by Alan Houel –
ISBN 0-85969-682-0
Dealing With People You Can't Stand by Dr. Rick Brinkman and
Dr. Rick Kirschner – **ISBN 0-07-007-838-6**
How to Work for an Idiot by John Hoover – **ISBN 1-56414-704-5**

MENTAL ENERGY

Cognitive Behavioural Therapy for Dummies by Rob Wilson and Rhena Branch – **ISBN 0-470-01838-0**

The Mind Gym by Octavius Black and Sebastian Bailey – **ISBN 0-316-72992-2**

Change Your Life in Seven Days by Paul McKenna – **ISBN 0-593-05055-X**

Awaken the Giant Within, **an audio book** by Anthony Robbins – **ISBN 0-671-58208-9**

Shift Happens by Robert Holden – **ISBN 0-34071688-6**

How High Can You Bounce? by Roger Crawford – **ISBN 0-09-181719-6**

Unleash Your True Potential, **a CD which includes relaxation techniques** by Glenn Harrold – **ISBN 1-901923-38-X**

Power Up Your Mind by Bill Lucas – **ISBN1-85788-275-X**

SPIRIT ENERGY

The Seven Spiritual Laws of Success by Deepak Chopra – **ISBN 0-593-04083-X**

A Return to Love by Marianne Williamson – **ISBN 0-7225-3299-7**

Corporate Head, Spiritual Heart by Shilpa Unalkat – **ISBN 978-0-9552028-0-3**

Care Packages for the Workplace by Barbara A. Glanz – **ISBN 0-07-024267-4**

PERSONAL UNDERSTANDING AND MANAGEMENT

The Seven Habits of Highly Effective People by Stephen Covey – **ISBN 0-684-85839-8**

The 8th Habit by Stephen Covey – **ISBN 0-684-84665-9**

How to Win Friends and Influence People by Dale Carnegie – **ISBN 0-671-72365-0**

Body Language by Allan Pease – **ISBN 0-85969-782-7**

PERSPECTIVE AND INSPIRATION
Successful But Something Missing by Ben Renshaw –
ISBN 0-7126-7053-X
Together But Something Missing by Ben Renshaw –
ISBN 0-0918-5593-4
Man's Search for Meaning by Viktor Frankl – **ISBN 0-671-02337-3**
If This is a Man by Primo Levi – **ISBN 0-349-10013-6**
Daily Reflections for Highly Effective People by Stephen Covey –
ISBN 0-671-88717-3
Your Best Year Yet by Jinny Ditzler – **ISBN 0-7225-3034-X**

GENERAL STRESS MANAGEMENT
Don't Sweat the Small Stuff at Work by Richard Carson –
ISBN 0-340-74873-7
Thrive on Stress by Jan Sutton – **ISBN 1-85703-554-2**
Stress Free Living by Dr. Trevor Powell – **ISBN 0-7513-0838-2**

RELAXATION
Calm at Work by Paul Wilson – **ISBN 0-14-026064-1**
The Calm Technique by Paul Wilson – **ISBN 0-72253626-7**
Total Relaxation by John R. Harvey PhD – **ISBN 1-56836-224-2**
Experience Yoga Nidra, **a CD** by Swami Janakananda –
ISBN 91-630-9488-6
**Music for relaxation – try www.solitudes.com and
www.somersetent.com/store where you can listen to music clips.
Also, slow baroque music of around 60 beats per minute is known
to slow heart rate and brain waves.**

WORK–LIFE BALANCE
First Things First by Stephen Covey and A. Roger Merrill –
ISBN 0-671-71283-7
Balancing Work and Life by Ben Renshaw and Robert Holden –
ISBN 0-7513-3365-4

Index